LAST DANCE AT DUM DUM

by Ayub Khan-Din

First performance at the New Ambassadors Theatre
West Street, London WC2 on 8 July 1999

Presented by:

Royal Court Theatre
St Martins Lane, WC2N 4BG
Tel: 0171 565 5000 Fax: 0171 565 5001

Ambassador Theatre Group
25 Shaftesbury Avenue, W1V 7HA
Tel: 0171 494 0333 Fax: 0171 494 0034

Guy Chapman Productions Ltd.
1-2 Henrietta Street, WC2E 8PS
Tel: 0171 379 7474 Fax: 0171 379 8484

Mark Goucher
35-39 Old Street, EC1
Tel: 0171 439 1589 Fax: 0171 439 1590

Last Dance at Dum Dum will tour to the following venues:

1st September	Theatre Royal, Newcastle
7th September	Liverpool Everyman
14th September	Malvern Theatre
21st September	Richmond Theatre
28th September	Theatre Royal, Brighton
12th October	Warwick Arts Centre
19th October	Lyceum, Sheffield

Last Dance at Dum Dum

by Ayub Khan-Din

Cast in order of appearance

Muriel Marsh Madhur Jaffrey
Daphne Willows Avril Elgar
Elliot Mukherjee Paul Bazely
Violet Wallis Sheila Burrell
Mr Jones Rashid Karapiet
Mr Chakravatty Madhav Sharma
Bertie Marsh Nicholas Le Prevost
Lydia Buller-Hughes Diana Fairfax

Director Stuart Burge
Designer Tim Hatley
Lighting Designer Mark Henderson
Sound Designer John Leonard and Frank Bradley for Aura Sound
Assistant Designer Stuart Nunn
Associate Costume Designer Lucy Roberts
Casting Lisa Makin and Julia Horan
Production Manager Jon Howes
Company Stage Manager Rob Young
Deputy Stage Manager Pea Horsley
Stage Management Julie Issott
Set Construction and Painting Souvenier
Props Buyer Kirsten Shiell
Press Peter Thompson Associates

The Producers would like to thank the following for their help with this production:
Lever Brothers for Wardrobe care, Ray Marsden Wig Studios, Lawrence at The Royal National Theatre
Armoury, Starship London Ltd 0181 208 2099 for stars, Francis Alexander, Lisa Popham, Paul Spyker,
Stratford East, Tamasha Theatre Company, Jonathan Mountford, The Press Department of the High
Commission of India, Honeyrose Products Ltd., Stowmarket for Herbal Smoking Mix, Parker Pen
Company, Jake Binnington.

MAROONED IN INDIA: THE ANGLO-INDIANS

At the end of the 15th century when Europeans and Indians first came in contact with each other a new community was created, known today as Anglo-Indian. At that time there was no defined way to describe the children of mixed descent who had never had an obvious position in Indian society and were known by a wide variety of names: Half Caste, Half-Breed, Indo-European, Indo Britain, East Indian and Euroasian. Now the term Anglo-Indian is officially defined in the Constitution of India of 1949 as meaning "...a person whose father or any other male progenitors in the male line is or was of European descent but who is domiciled within the territory of India..."

Due to shifts in political dominance, people of mixed descent are often confronted with the inevitable choice between the two different cultural backgrounds from which they originate. The Anglo-Indians have always had a preference for their European origin, even today, although it has become less important compared with the first centuries of their existence. Their mother tongue is English and their religion Christianity.

Once a flourishing community in most of India's railway colonies and metropolitan towns, Anglo-Indians in the country became a fast-declining minority with the end of the British Raj. Mass migrations to Britain, Canada and Australia took their toll of the all but stateless group, leaving behind less than 100,000 of the estimated 250,000 Anglo-Indian population at Independence. The ones that remained were to a large extent the old and infirm, people incapable of making their way in the West.

Although left behind in the exodus, the Anglo-Indian old are not entirely homeless today. Lacking the security of the joint family, Anglo-Indians had to set up a series of old people's homes to take care of their aged, to which the last remnants of their culture now flock.

Although they are India's only community with 100% literacy, few Anglo-Indians adjusted to the new way of life after Independence. The minuscule ethnic group rapidly lost the privileges it had enjoyed under the British rulers and found itself increasingly isolated in free India.

Extracts from India Today, August 1 - 15, 1981 and The International Journal of Anglo-Indian Studies. http://elecpress.monash.edu.au/ijais/introd~1.html.

THE COMPANY

Ayub Khan-Din (writer)

Last Dance At Dum Dum is Ayub's second Royal Court production.
Also for the Royal Court with the Tamasha Theatre Company: East Is East (Royal Court Theatre Upstairs & Downstairs, Theatre Royal Stratford East, Tour.
Other theatre includes: East is East (Manhattan Theatre Club, New York, Oldham Coliseum.)
Films Include: East Is East which was recently shown at the Cannes Film Festival 1999.
Awards Include: 1997 Writers' Guild Awards for Best New West End Play, Best New Writer, 1997 John Whiting Award. (East Is East).

Paul Bazely

For the Royal Court with Tamasha Theatre Company: East Is East (Royal Court Theatre Upstairs and Downstairs, Theatre Royal Stratford East, Tour)
Other theatre includes: The Big Heart, Soldiers (Contact); Brother Eichmann, Beauty and the Beast (Manchester Library); Richard III, Haroun and the Sea of Stories (RNT); Cigarettes and Chocolate, Bye Bye Blues, Selling Out, Tomfoolery (Scarborough); Macbeth (Full Company); Peter Pan, Toad of Toad Hall (Birmingham Rep); A Servant of Two Masters (Sheffield); A Tainted Dawn (Tamasha Tour).
Television Includes: Heartbeat, New Voices - The Quiet Life, Emmerdale, Medics, Casualty, Resnick & Resnick II, Making Out, Wuthering Heights.
Radio Includes: Grease Monkeys, The Burning Glass, Westway, Resnick, Not All Angels Have Wings, No Problem, The Maneater of Malgudi.
Film: See Red.

Stuart Burge (director)

Stuart was Artistic Director of the Royal Court 1976 - 1979 and of Nottingham Playhouse from 1968 - 1974.
For the Royal Court: Fair Slaughter, The London Cuckolds (also Lyric, Hammersmith).
Other theatre includes: The Father (Tour); Hobson's Choice, Sunsets and Glories (West Yorkshire Playhouse); Another Country, The Black Prince (West End); The Ruling Class, Lulu (Nottingham Playhouse & West End); The Devil is an Ass, Measure For Measure (Edinburgh Festival/RNT); Richard II, Henry IV Parts I & II (Stratford, Ontario); The Workhouse Donkey by John Arden (Chichester).
Opera Includes: La Colombe by Gounod (Buxton and Sadler's Wells).
Television Includes: Talking Heads with Alan Bennett, Thora Hird, and Eileen Atkins; The Wexford Trilogy, After The Dance, House Of Bernarda Alba, The Rainbow, David Copperfield, The Power and the Glory, Under Western Eyes, Sons And Lovers, School for Scandal, Much Ado About Nothing, Importance Of Being Earnest, Bill Brand, Uncle Vanya, The Philanthropist, The Old Men at the Zoo.
Film Includes: Julius Caesar, Othello, Naming the Names.

Sheila Burrell

For the Royal Court: Salonika
Other theatre includes: Richard III, King John (RSC); School for Scandal, Richard II, Macbeth, Absolute Hell (RNT); The Bacchae (Actors Company); Bartholomew Fair (The Roundhouse); Mother Dear (The Ambassadors), Exit The King (Lyric, Hammersmith); Great Expectations, Marya (Old Vic); Everything in the Garden (Palace, Watford); Nana (Mermaid); Little Eyolf (Orange Tree); The Handyman (Chichester).
Television includes: The Six Wives of Henry VIII, Love Lies Bleeding, Anna Karenina, Frost in May, The Tribute, Radio Pictures, Lizzie's Pictures, Gaudy Night, The Trial of Klaus Barbie, Brush Strokes, The Intercom Conspiracy, Devices and Desires, The Darling Buds of May, Young Indiana, Cold Comfort Farm, Bramwell III, Hetty Wainthrop Investigates, The Bill, Casualty, Trial and Retribution III.
Film includes: Afraid Of The Dark, Jane Eyre, Woodlanders.

Avril Elgar

For the Royal Court: Sport of My Mad Mother, Epitaph For George Dillon, Three Sisters, The Voysey Inheritance, Ruffian on the Stair.
Theatre includes: Stanley, Half Life, Inner Voices (RNT); The Corn Is Green, Hope against Hope, Great Expectations, Admirable Crichton, Death of a Salesman, The Glass Menagerie, Pride And Prejudice, The Importance of Being Earnest, A Family Reunion, Court in the Act, Amongst Barbarians (Royal Exchange Theatre, Manchester); Phedre (Almeida at Albery

Television Includes: Under The Skin, Winnie, The Citadel, Thirteen for Dinner Paying Guests, Children of Dynemouth, The Late Show, Casualty, George & Mildred, The Bill, Tales Of The Unexpected, A Taste For Death, Goodnight Mister Tom.
Radio Includes: Little Dorrit, Our Mutal Friend, The Daughter-In-Law, Dombey And Son.

Diana Fairfax
Theatre includes: 'Tis Pity She's a Whore (Nottingham Playhouse); Man & Superman (Arena Theatre, Tour); A Month of Sundays (Cambridge Theatre); A Streetcar Named Desire (Queen's Theatre, Hornchurch); Hay Fever (Tour); Let's Murder Vivaldi (King's Head); Ring Round The Moon, Skin of Our Teeth (Library Theatre, Manchester); You Never Can Tell (Yvonne Arnaud Theatre, Guildford); Private Members (Bush); Heartbreak House (Lyceum, Edinburgh); Death of a Salesman (Crucible, Sheffield); Two Gentlemen of Verona, Bartholomew Fair (Open Air Theatre, Regent's Park); King's Rhapsody (Churchill Theatre, Bromley); Cherry Orchard (Haymarket, Basingstoke); Long Day's Journey into Night (Theatre Royal, Northampton); Summer of the 17th Doll (Birmingham Rep); Tango at The End Of Winter (Lyceum, Edinburgh / Piccadilly Theatre); Come Blow Your Horn (The Mill at Sonning); The Ghost Sonata (Gate); Outward Bound (Palace, Watford).
Television Includes: Bleak House, Emma, Traitor, Just Wiliam, Love in a Cold Climate, Portrait of a Marriage, Casualty, Hard Times, How Do You Want Me?

Tim Hatley (designer)
For the Royal Court: Harry and Me
Other theatre includes: Sleep With Me, Darker Face of the Earth, The Caucasian Chalk Circle, Antony & Cleopatra, Flight, Stanley (RNT); Richard III, Goodnight Children Everywhere, Talk Of The City (RSC); Mr Puntila & His Man Matti (Tour, co-production with The Right Size), The Play About The Baby, Chatsky (Almeida); The Maids (Donmar Warehouse); Suddenly Last Summer (Comedy Theatre); The Three Lives of Lucie Cabrol, Out of a House Walked a Man (Theatre de Complicité); The Nose (Nottingham Playhouse); Moscow Stations, Reader, Poor Superman (Traverse Theatre); The Misunderstanding, Damned For Despair (Gate Theatre).
Opera Includes: Carmen, Orpheus in the Underworld, The Return Of Ulyses (Opera North); H.M.S. Pinafore, Die Fledermaus (D'Oyly Carte Opera) Il Trovatore, Ariadne Auf Naxos (Scottish Opera); Les Miserables (Gothenburg Opera); Andrea Chenier (Karlstad Opera, Sweden).
Dance Includes: Roughcut (Rambert Dance Company); Cinderella (NBT); Unrequited Moments (ENB).
Awards include: Olivier Award for Best Designer for Stanley (RNT); London Evening Standard Award nomination for Mr Puntila and his Man Matti (Almeida); a Time Out Award, the Plays and Players Critics' Award for Best Designer and the Linbury Prize for Stage Design. He also represented Britain in the Prague Quadrennial Exhibition of Theatre Design.

Mark Henderson (lighting designer)
Theatre Includes: Hamlet, The Judas Kiss, No Man's Land, The Deep Blue Sea, Naked, Heartbreak House, Ivanov, The Government Inspector, Phedre, Britannicus, The Iceman Cometh, Vassa, Plenty (Almeida); Cat On A Hot Tin Roof, The Shaughraun, Hamlet, Sunday in the Park with George, Long Day's Journey into Night, Pygmalion, Racing Demon, Sweet Bird Of Youth, A Little Night Music, The Cripple Of Inishmaan, The Oedipus Plays, Amy's View, Copenhagen, The Forest (RNT); Follies, Carmen Jones, Neville's Island, Indian Ink, Passion, Amy's View, Which Witch, Girlfriends Budgie, The Rink, Mutiny, Kiss Me Kate, Gasping, Suddenly Last Summer; Steve Coogan, West Side Story, Grease Is The Word (West End). Mark has also lit productions for ENO, Royal Opera, WNO, Scottish Opera, Glyndebourne Festival Opera, and for the Royal Ballet, LCDT, Rambert Dance Company, Scottish Ballet and Northern Ballet.
Television Includes: Rowan Atkinson in Boston, Under Milk Wood.
Film Includes: The Tall Guy.

Madhur Jaffrey
Theatre includes: The Guide (Broadway); Conduct Unbecoming (Ethel Barrymore Theatre, NY); Shakuntala (St Mark's Theatre, NY); King Of The Dark Chamber (Jan Hus Theatre, NY); A Tenth of an Inch Makes the Difference (Off Broadway); My Ancestor's House (Theatre for the New City, NY); Two Rooms (The Signature Theater, NY); Medea (Lyric, Hammersmith)
Television includes: Peacock Spring, Firm Friends, Lovematch, A Wanted Man, The Bloodless

Theatre); The Innocents (Greenwich Theatre); Blithe Spirit, Macbeth (Bristol Old Vic).
Arena, The Nurses, US Steel, The Jack Benny Show.
Film includes: The Assam Garden, Heat and Dust, Autobiography of a Princess, Guru,
Shakespeare Wallah, Six Degrees Of Separation, Wolf, Vanya On 42nd Street, Flawless.
Awards Include: Silver Bear Best Actress Award at the Berlin International Film Festival for
Shakespeare Wallah.

Rashid Karapiet
Theatre includes: Indian Ink (Aldwych); My Native Land (Lyric Studio, Hammersmith); Life &
Loves Of Mr Patel (Leicester Haymarket); Table of the Horseman (Greenwich Theatre); A
Kind Of Immigrant (Graeae Touring); Untouchable (Tamasha Theatre Company); The Indian
wants the Bronx (RNT Platform); A Passage to India (Oxford Playhouse/Comedy).
Television Includes: The Waiting Time, Mrs Merton and Malcolm, The Creatives, A Wing and
a Prayer, Peak Practice, Between The Lines, Cardiac Arrest, The Bill, Pie in the Sky, Family
Pride, Tandoori Nights.
Radio Includes: Tughlaq, Untouchable, Badal and His Bike, Man-Eater of Malgudi, Citizens,
Strangers in Paradise.
Film Includes: Jinnah, Chambre à Part, Paris By Night, Water, Foreign Body, A Passage to
India.

Nicholas Le Prevost
For the Royal Court: The Strip, The Glad Hand, Seven Lears.
Other theatre includes: Amadeus (Old Vic); The Prime of Miss Jean Brodie (RNT); A Winter's
Tale, The Maid's Tragedy (Globe); Hedda Gabler (Chichester / Tour); Mind Millie for Me
(Haymarket Theatre Royal/Tour); Privates on Parade (Greenwich Theatre / Tour); An
Absolute Turkey (Gielgud); Tartuffe (Playhouse); Blues for Mister Charlie (Royal Exchange,
Manchester); Two Way Mirror (Nottingham Playhouse).
Television includes: The Vicar of Dibley, Up the Garden Path, The Camomile Lawn, The Great
Paperchase, Stolen, The Imitation Game, The Borgias, It Takes a Worried Man, Jewel in the
Crown, Harnessing Peacocks, Inspector Morse, The Midsomer Murders.
Film includes: Clockwise, Letters from the East, Land Girls, Cold Enough for Snow,
Shakespeare in Love, Being Considered, Whatever Happened to Harold Smith.
Recent radio includes: Albertina by Howard Barker, Frozen Images by Kristian Smeds,
Babblewick Hall by Scott Cherry.

Madhav Sharma
For the Royal Court: No One Was Saved
Other theatre includes: Indian Ink (Aldwych); Crazyhorse (BAC / UK Tour); Not Just an
Asian Babe (Watermans); Untold Secret of Aspi (Cockpit); Worlds Apart, House of the Sun
(Theatre Royal Stratford East); Blithe Spirit (Birmingham Rep); Twelfth Night (Dundee Rep);
Romeo and Juliet (Albany Empire); Therese Raquin (Nottingham Playhouse); Romeo and
Juliet (Shaw Theatre and UK Tour/Edinburgh Festival, New York State University); Fiddler on
the Roof (UK Tour); Hamlet (The Howff); Baby Love (Soho Poly); High Diplomacy
(Westminster Theatre); The Importance of Being Neutral (ICA); Twelfth Night, The Hollow
Crown (Theatre Royal, Lincoln); Hindle Wakes, Alfie, How are you Johnny?, An Inspector
Calls, The Caretaker, September Tide, Mr Kettle and Mrs Moon, The Poker Session, A
Murder has been Arranged, A Taste of Honey (Casino Theatre, Southport), Captain
Carvalho, England Our England (Victoria Theatre, Salford); Twelfth Night, The Proposal, A
Midsummer Night's Dream (UK Schools Tour); Othello, Twelfth Night, The Merchant of
Venice, Henry V (International Tours).
Television includes: Dream Team, Bugs, Trial and Retribution, McCallum, Captain Colenzo's
Last Voyage, Inspector Alleyn, The Rector's Wife, Amongst Barbarians, Tygo Road, Cardiac
Arrest, Do the Right Thing, The Rhythm of Raz, Black and Blue, Fighting Back, Medics, Boon,
This Office Life, The Bill, South of the Border, King and Castle, Shalom Salaam, Tandoori
Nights, Old Men at the Zoo, Maybury, Minder, Target, The Road to 1984, Blunt Instrument,
Cold Warrior, Sarah, Public Eye, Crown Court, Juliet Bravo, Uncle Sangi, Imperial Palace,
Singh 171, Adam Smith, Coronation Street, The Brahmin Widow, First Lady, Moonbase 3,
Doctor Who, Anything but the Woods, Rogues Rock, The Moonstone, Uncle Tulip, Angels,
Basil Brush Show, Harriet's Back in Town, The Sweeney, One for the Road, Kipling, The
Newcomers.
Films include: East is East, Entrapment, Such a Long Journey, Wild West, Giro City, Shadey,
The Euphoric Scale, Change of Life, The Awakening, Marriages, Tangled Web, Up the Front.

PRODUCERS

The English Stage Company at the Royal Court Theatre

The English Stage Company was formed to bring serious writing back to the stage. The first Artistic Director, George Devine, wanted to create a vital and popular theatre. He encouraged new writing that explored subjects drawn from contemporary life as well as pursuing European plays and forgotten classics. When John Osborne's Look Back in Anger was first produced in 1956 it forced British Theatre into the modern age. Early Court Writers included Arnold Wesker, John Arden, Ann Jellicoe, Edward Bond and David Storey. They were followed by David Hare, Howard Brenton, Caryl Churchill, Timberlake Wertenbaker, Robert Holman and Jim Cartwright. In the 1990s the Royal Court has produced a new generation of playwrights, including Conor McPherson, Jez Butterworth, Martin McDonagh, Ayub Khan-Din, Joe Penhall, Nick Grosso, Rebecca Prichard, Sarah Kane, Mark Ravenhill and other young writers.

Many established playwrights had their early plays produced in the Theatre Upstairs including Anne Devlin, Andrea Dunbar, Sarah Daniels, Jim Cartwright, Clare McIntyre, Winsome Pinnock, Martin Crimp and Phyllis Nagy. Theatre Upstairs productions regularly transfer to the Theatre Downstairs, as with Ariel Dorfman's Death and the Maiden, Sebastian Barry's The Steward of Christendom (a co-production with Out of Joint); Martin McDonagh's The Beauty Queen of Leenane (a co-production with Druid Theatre Company), Ayub Khan-Din's East is East (a co-production with Tamasha Theatre Company). 1992 - 1999 have been record-breaking years at the box office with capacity houses for Death and the Maiden, Six Degrees of Separation, Oleanna, Hysteria, The Cavalcaders, The Kitchen, The Queen and I, The Libertine, Simpatico, Mojo, The Steward of Christendom, The Beauty Queen of Leenane, East is East, The Chairs and The Weir.

After four decades the Royal Court's aims remain consistent with thoses established by George Devine. The Royal Court is still a major focus in the country for the production of new work. Scores of plays first seen at the Royal Court are now part of the national and international dramatic repertoire.

Ambassador Theatre Group

Ambassador Theatre Group Ltd (ATG) has three main areas of activity: the ownership and management of theatre buildings, theatre production (in the West End but also nationally and internationally) and the development of new productions.

ATG currently owns and operates the following arts buildings: The Duke of Yorks and the Ambassadors in London, The New Victoria Theatre and Ambassadors Cinemas in Woking, The Victoria Hall and Regent Theatre in Stoke-on-Trent, The Milton Keynes Theatre and the historic Theatre Royal Brighton in June.

ATG and its management company the Turnstyle Group Ltd., has a considerable track record in producing and co-producing for the West End and on national and international tours. Recent productions include: Carmen Jones, The Rocky Horror Show, Smokey Joe's Cafe, A Chorus Line, Slava's Snow Show, The Late Middle Classes and the Royal Court's Olivier Award winning play The Weir. Currently in rehearsal is the first revival in 40 years of the fifties musical The Pajama Game and a new musical celebrating soul music, Soul Train.

In 1998 Sonia Friedman joined the Ambassador Theatre Group as Producer where she is responsible for initiating, developing and producing a wide range of work for theatres across the West End, UK and internationally. From 1989-1993 Sonia was head of Mobile Productions and Theatre for Young People at the RNT where she was responsible for producing over 30 productions and projects. In 1993 Sonia co-founded Out of Joint with Max Stafford-Clark. Co-productions with the Royal Court, RNT and Hampstead include The Queen and I by Sue Townsend, The Libertine by Stephen Jeffreys, The Steward of Christendom by Sebastian Barry, The Break of Day by Timberlake Wertenbaker, The Positive Hour by April de Angelis, Shopping and Fucking by Mark Ravenhill, Our Lady of Sligo by Sebastian Barry and Blue Heart by Caryl Churchill. She has also produced The Man of Mode, Road and Three Sisters at the Royal Court, and Our Country's Good. In 1994 Sonia also produced Maria Friedman by Special Arrangement at the Donmar Warehouse.

Guy Chapman

Guy Chapman was head of marketing for the Royal Court Theatre for seven years. In 1994 he formed Guy Chapman Associates and a subsidiary, Chapman Duncan Productions Ltd., to produce and tour new work. This company premiered with Phyllis Nagy's Disappeared, touring for seven weeks as well as playing at the Royal Court Theatre Upstairs. This was followed by Andrew Alty's Something About Us at the Lyric Hammersmith Studio in 1995 and Godfrey Hamilton's Road Movie (Lyric Hammersmith and tour, 1996).

Guy Chapman co-produced Brothers of the Brush at the Arts Theatre in 1996 and Martin and John at the Bush Theatre in 1998.

In 1996 Guy Chapman and Paul Spyker launched Bright Ltd and have produced: James Edwin Parker's Two Boys on a Cold Winter's Night, John Logan's Never the Sinner, Dan Rebellato's Showstopper and The Twilight of the Golds by Jonathan Tolins, all at the Arts Theatre; and Stephen Schwartz's musical Pippin at The Bridewell Theatre.

With G & J Productions, Bright Ltd has co-produced Mark Ravenhill's Shopping and Fucking (Gielgud / Queen's / National tour / New York Theatre Workshop). They also co-produced Jackie Clune's Chicks with Flicks (The King's Head / Tour) and Enda Walsh's Disco Pigs (The Arts Theatre).

Recent co-productions: Crave by Sarah Kane (Chelsea Centre, Traverse, Royal Court Theatre, Berlin Festival and Dublin Festival); Jackie Clune's It's Jackie! (Assembly Rooms Edinburgh / The Drill Hall / National Tour); Sea Urchins (Grace Theatre); Love Upon the Throne (Assembly Rooms, Edinburgh, Oxford Playhouse, Bush Theatre, Comedy Theatre); The Snowman (Peacock Theatre); Frantic Assembly's Sell Out (with Mark Goucher and Paul Spyker); Holy Mothers (New Ambassadors Theatre with the Royal Court).

Current productions include: Chicks with Flicks in the USA and Austria, The Snowman at The Peacock in November 1999 and an adaptation of Oscar Moore's PWA with Fierce Earth.

Mark Goucher

In 1997 Mark was the joint recipient of The Stage / Barclays Award for special achievement in Regional Theatre and over the last eleven years has co-produced ground breaking productions in the West End.

For the last six years Mark has successfully represented the Reduced Shakespeare Company's productions in the UK with The Complete Works of Shakespeare (abridged) and The Complete History of America (abridged) now in their fourth year at the Criterion Theatre. The Reduced Shakespeare Company has also toured extensively with The Bible, The Complete Word of God (abridged) and, in the autumn, their new show Millennium the Musical.

West End co-productions and subsequent tours include: Trainspotting, Shopping and Fucking, Fever Pitch, Steven Berkoff in One Man, Anorak of Fire, Ennio Marchetto and Kit and the Widow. Touring co-productions include Think No Evil of Us: My Life with Kenneth Williams, An Audience with George Melly, Poulter and Duff and Graham Norton.

Mark is also involved as a co-producer in the New Ambassadors' inaugural season with productions of Holy Mothers by Werner Schwab and Sell Out by Frantic Assembly.

FOR THE ROYAL COURT THEATRE

FOR NEW AMBASSADORS THEATRE

Producer	Sonia Friedman
Head of Operations	David Blyth
Theatre Administrator	Tim Brunsden
Marketing	Shereden Mathews
	Lisa Popham for Dewynters
Production Assistant	Amanda Murray
Trainee Producer	Wade Kamaria
Acting Deputy Manager	Rachel Fisher
Chief LX	Matthew O'Conner
Deputy LX	Michelle Green
Master Carpenter	Ivan Smith
Deputy Carpenter	Kevin Hough
Personnel Officer	Maxi Harvey
Finance Consultant	Judy Burridge
Personnel Administrator	Debbie Hill
Accountant	Caroline Abrahams
Maintenance Technician	Martin Hammond
Stage Door Keeper	Ben Till
Relief Stage Door Keeper	Sam Becker

AMBASSADORS THEATRE GROUP BOARD OF DIRECTORS

Chairman	Eddie Kulukundis OBE
Deputy Chairman	Peter Beckwith
	David Beresford-Jones
	Howard Panter
	Rosemary Squire
	Miles Wilkin

FOR GUY CHAPMAN ASSOCIATES

Matthew Bartlett
Guy Chapman
Steven Drew
Jenny Eldridge
Ryan Levitt
Sally Lycett
Michael Parke
Bonnie Royal
Jonathan Russell
Naomi Sherrez

FOR MARK GOUCHER

General Manager	Sid Higgins
Production Manager	Paul Lamont
Accounts Manager	Janne Winhede

RE-BUILDING THE ROYAL COURT

The Royal Court was thrilled in 1995 to be awarded a National Lottery grant through the Arts Council of England, to pay for three quarters of a £26 million project to completely re-build our 100-year old home. The rules of the award required the Royal Court to raise £7 million as partnership funding.

Thanks to the generous support of the donors listed below and a recent major donation from the Jerwood Foundation, we have very nearly reached the target. The building work is near completion at the Sloane Square site and the theatre is due to re-open in Autumn 1999.

With only £100,000 left to raise, each donation makes a significant difference to the realisation of this exciting project. If you would like to help, or for further information, please contact Royal Court Development on 0171 565 5050.

ROYAL COURT DEVELOPMENT BOARD
Elisabeth Murdoch (Chair), Jonathan Cameron (Vice Chair), Timothy Burrill, Anthony Burton, Jonathan Caplin QC, Victoria Elenowitz, Monica Gerard-Sharp, Feona McEwan, Michael Potter, Sue Stapely, Charlotte Watcyn Lewis

RE-BUILDING SUPPORTERS INCLUDE:
Jerwood Foundation

WRITERS CIRCLE
BSkyB Ltd
Foundation for Sport and the Arts
News International plc
Pathé
The Eva and Hans K Rausing Trust
The Rayne Foundation
Garfield Weston Foundation

DIRECTORS CIRCLE
The Esmée Fairbairn Charitable Trust
The Granada Group plc
John Lewis Partnership plc

ACTORS CIRCLE
City Parochial Foundation
Quercus Charitable Trust
RSA Art for Architecture Award Scheme
The Basil Samuel Charitable Trust
The Trusthouse Charitable Foundation
The Woodward Charitable Trust

For information about the American Friends of the Royal Court Theatre telephone 001 212 946 5724.

PROGRAMME SUPPORTERS

The Royal Court (English Stage Company Ltd) is supported financially by a wide range of private companies and public bodies. The company receives its principal funding from the Arts Council of England. The Royal Borough of Kensington & Chelsea gives an annual grant to the Royal Court Young Writers' Programme and the London Boroughs Grants Committee contributes to the cost of productions in its Theatre Upstairs. Major sponsors, foundations and individual supporters include the following:

TRUSTS AND FOUNDATIONS
A.S.K. Theater Projects, LA
Bulldog Princep Theatrical Fund
Jerwood Foundation
John Lyons Charity
The Peggy Ramsay Foundation
Alan & Babette Sainsbury Charitable Fund
The John Studzinski Foundation

SPONSORS
The Austrian Cultural Institute
Barclays Bank plc
Bloomberg News
The Granada Group plc
Guiding Star Ltd (Jerusalem)
Virgin Atlantic
Business Members
American Airlines
AT&T (UK) Ltd
British Interactive Broadcasting Ltd
BSkyB
Channel Four Television
Davis Polk & Wardwell
Deep End Design
Goldman Sachs International
Heidrick & Struggles
Lambie-Nairn
Lazard Brothers & Co. Ltd
Lee and Pemberton
Mishcon de Reya Solicitors
OgilvyOne
Redwood Publishing plc
Simons Muirhead & Burton
Sullivan & Cromwell
J Walter Thompson

INDIVIDUAL MEMBERS
Patrons
Advanpress
Associated Newspapers Ltd
Gill Carrick
Citigate Communications
Greg Dyke
Homevale Ltd
Laporte plc
Lex Service plc
Barbara Minto
New Penny Productions Ltd
A T Poeton & Son Ltd

LAST DANCE AT DUM DUM

To
BUKI

This play is about Anglo-Indians, a community which traces
its ancestry over the two hundred-year presence of the British
in India: a community which is very proud of that connection
and still to this day celebrates that fact. They are a separate
community and as such are represented by their own M.P.s
in the Indian parliament. Since the end of British rule and
partition of India, many Anglo-Indians decided to leave the
sub-continent and there are communities in Australia, Canada,
and in England.

Many Anglo-Indians are European in appearance and can pass
as such; indeed some are ashamed of their Indian ancestry.
In view of this I feel strongly that directors should consider
casting both European as well as Asian actors in these roles.

Ayub Khan-Din,
February 1999

4

Characters

MURIEL MARSH

DAPHNE WILLOWS

VIOLET WALLIS

BERTIE MARSH

MR JONES

CHAKRAVATTY

ELLIOT

LYDIA BULLER-HUGHES

This playscript went to press before the opening night and may therefore differ slightly from the text as performed.

ACT ONE

Scene One

Morning, Calcutta 1981. We are in the front garden of a large colonial bungalow. The house stands stage left, its grandeur long since peeled away with the paint from its once white walls. The house has a verandah, on which are chairs. On the lawn stands some old garden furniture with a dishevelled-looking umbrella above a table. The garden has been well cared for, but there is a decayed look about the place, bald patches on the lawn etc. Upstage is a jasmine-covered wall that divides this house from the one beyond. Rising above the wall in the next garden we see a large flagpole that almost dominates the set. Up-stage right, there are gates which lead onto the street. From offstage we can hear the sounds of India waking: constant car and bus horns, the cries of the vendors and the cawing of crows. Suddenly, we hear harsh, taped, martial music come from the house next door. A large orange flag rises up the flagpole to the cries of 'Jai Hind' from the people next door. A lot has been written about the Anglo-Indian accent, some say it's very similar to the Welsh accent. This is a recipe for disaster and should be avoided at all costs. I suggest that BERTIE, MURIEL, and DAPHNE have pukka Indian-English accents and that MR JONES, VIOLET and ELLIOT have thicker versions.

The door of the bungalow suddenly bursts open, and out rushes what looks like a screaming banshee. MURIEL ROBERTS, 66, Anglo-Indian, long grey hair a dishevelled mess around her shoulders, night-dress flapping behind her. In her hands she carries a jug of water, which she throws over the wall. She then proceeds to throw anything over that comes to hand, which at this moment is the umbrella from the lawn.

MURIEL. Stop! Stop! Stop it you Pandy bastards! You bloody turncoats! Don't stop there, come and slit our throats in the night like the bloody sneak thieves you are! Come on, rape me now while I have this bloody umbrella in my hands, you fainthearted bastards!

Behind her from the house rushes another woman in her night-dress. DAPHNE WILLOWS, 67, Anglo Indian. She rushes over to MURIEL and tries to pull her away from the wall.

DAPHNE. Muriel! You mustn't do that, come away. You'll get us into trouble again you silly girl. Mr Jones! Bertie!

Around the corner of the bungalow appears ELLIOT. Late twenties/early thirties, a skinny, beanpole-like creature with long hair. He wears very tight trousers and a Kurta shirt. He stops and begins to laugh hysterically at the antics of MURIEL, who is now trying to scale the wall with DAPHNE hanging onto her legs.

DAPHNE. Well don't just stand there laughing like a demented fakir you bloody mutt. Fetch Mr Jones! Muriel, do come down, there's a dear, you'll frighten Mr Chakravatty and his friends.

MURIEL. This has to stop, it has to, I know where it'll lead. Murderers of peace! Don't think I don't know what you're up to!

ELLIOT finds this even more hysterical.

DAPHNE. Elliot! Mr Jones now!

ELLIOT runs off through the house still laughing. DAPHNE is still struggling with MURIEL.

MURIEL. Come on, I'll fight you, you bloody bastards! I'm my father's daughter. Long live free India! Down with communalism!

VIOLET WALLIS, 70, Anglo-Indian comes out of the house, her hair is scraped back off her face and she wears an old floral patterned dress.

VIOLET. Remember the Black Hole! Remember Cawnpore!

> VIOLET *goes off through the gates.*

DAPHNE. Remember the mortgage dear. We're months in arrears, and I don't think Mr Chakravatty will be in any mood to be patient after this.

> DAPHNE *manages to pull* MURIEL *down from the wall but is still having trouble keeping hold of her as they scramble about on the grass.*

MURIEL. Oh for heavens sake Daphne, what do you think you're doing, let go. We have to let them know we protest. You can't just sit back and allow these things to happen. Why do you always have to take their side?

DAPHNE. Why don't you come and sit down Muriel and we'll have Elliot bring us our tea on the lawn. That'll be nice won't it?

MURIEL. Don't you bring that bugger near me, you don't know what you might catch. He's bloody queer you know.

DAPHNE. Oh, well now you're just being silly.

MURIEL. It's true, I've seen him, prancing around like a tart from some Bombay movie.

DAPHNE. Well he's all that we can afford, so he can do what he likes for all I care.

MURIEL. He dresses up in women's clothes you know. That's how Bertie found him. Flat on his back, legs akimbo, dressed as Marilyn Monroe with some Johnny in South Parks cemetery. No respect for the dead.

DAPHNE. Oh Muriel, please come and sit down.

MURIEL. He looks nothing like her of course, he doesn't have the movie star quality I had you see. It takes more than high heels and a pair of cheap nylons to reach the top in the movies. Help me up. You know, I could have been up there with the greats. I told you about that Hollywood fellow didn't I?

DAPHNE *leads* MURIEL *over to the chairs on the grass and sits her down.* MURIEL *sits and has become quite calm.* DAPHNE *starts to brush her down.*

DAPHNE. Oh, Muriel stop it. Just look at the state of you.

MURIEL. It's true. I was a bit of a beauty when I was younger, used to turn heads all the time. I worked at the Calcutta telephone exchange with Merle Oberon. Though she wasn't Merle Oberon the big film star then of course. No, she was one of us. Queenie Roberts, Queenie, ridiculous name. Another one of our pretensions, no wonder the British laughed at us. Anyway, we were both talent spotted and told that we had star quality, only mine was darker. Too dark. So, I stayed on at the telephone exchange and Queenie became a star. But what would I have done with Hollywood, when I have Dum Dum and you and Bertie and Violet and Mr Jones, (*She stands and shouts in the direction of next door.*) and that fat fascist bastard Chakravatty!

DAPHNE. Let's not forget Elliot.

MURIEL. Why not, he's a female impersonator and I'll have no truck with them.

From the house comes running MR JONES, *67, Anglo-Indian. He's dressed in a black suit, white shirt and black bow tie.* ELLIOT *is with him.*

JONES. What is it, what's happened!

DAPHNE. It's alright now Mr Jones, Muriel was having one of her turns, weren't you dear?

MURIEL. A what? Daphne, I'm not a child, don't patronise me. No Mr Jones, I wasn't having a turn I was protesting at the nonsense going on next door. It may have eventually turned into a turn, I don't know. I can't remember that well any more.

JONES. You're alright now though Mrs Marsh, or would you like us to send for the doctor? Where's Bertie?

MURIEL. I just want you all to stop fussing. Now if Elliot could bring me my tea, I'll consider my morning replete.

DAPHNE *and* MR JONES *look at each other. We hear a commotion from the street as* MR CHAKRAVATTY *waddles in. He's an overweight man in his sixties; he wears khaki trousers, a crisp white shirt and he carries a briefcase. In the other hand he carries the garden umbrella thrown over the wall by* MURIEL.

CHAKRA. Dear ladies, dear ladies, this really has got to stop. (*He holds up the umbrella.*) This missile nearly took out Mr Chopra's one good eye, he has an aged mother and ten children to look after. You would have left them bereft of the only breadwinner.

MURIEL. Sod off!

CHAKRA. You see what happens when I turn the other cheek! My people and I are still abused. Do you know what it took to stop my members from coming here and burning you out of house and home? Well do you? No, I don't think you do. I held them back Madam, me, Chakravatty the fascist!

MURIEL. You only held them back because you have us remortgaged up to our necks, you bloody fraud. Didn't want your thugs damaging your investment.

DAPHNE. I really must apologise Mr Chakravatty, you see she was having one of her turns, wasn't she Mr Jones?

JONES. Yes, quite terrible it was too . . .

DAPHNE. Violent, wouldn't you say Mr Jones?

MR JONES *is not sure if he can carry on the lie.*

JONES. Well, she was quite miffed.

CHAKRA. A man with my position in the community shouldn't be expected to have to put up with this behaviour. All I try to do is be fair to you. Have I mentioned your outstanding payments?

DAPHNE. We do appreciate it Mr Chakravatty, and the arrears will be paid as soon as possible. We just haven't found anyone to replace poor Mrs Gort yet.

MURIEL. You remember Mrs Gort? Well you should do, you drove her to an early grave.

DAPHNE. Muriel, that's absolute twaddle and no way to talk to Mr Chakravatty after he was so kind in offering us a loan. You ought to be thankful to him that we still have a roof over our heads. I can't say how sorry we are about these outbursts Mr Chakravatty, it's her illness . . .

MURIEL. Is it buggery!

CHAKRA. This is still no excuse for the insults my members and I receive from this woman. It's happening two or three times a week now Miss Willows. Are we to be persecuted for our beliefs in our own country?

MURIEL. Beliefs! You call that poison you spew out a belief, you Nazi bastard! Get out, go on, out! Before I take a bloody stick to you and really lose my temper. I put up with Nehru and his bloody congress wallahs, but I draw the line at female impersonators and Nazis. In that order.

CHAKRAVATTY *turns to* DAPHNE.

DAPHNE. Muriel, stop it right now.

CHAKRA. I'm a reasonable man, my associates are reasonable people, and we'd be willing to give you a good price for this property.

MURIEL. You see! You see, I told you the moment you took his bloody money he'd have his foot in the door.

CHAKRA. I can assure you that everything was legal and above board, Mrs Willows.

MURIEL. You'll not get this house while I'm alive! I know about your plans for a school, spread your poison to the young will you? I caught some of his acolytes digging about here the other day you know. Trespassing!

CHAKRA. We do have plans to build a school in the future it's true, but we're not intending to do anything underhand.

MURIEL. Don't believe a word he says Daphne.

CHAKRA. There's nothing sinister, you've always known this was my plan.

DAPHNE. You know we have no intention of moving anywhere Mr Chakravatty.

CHAKRA. My dear lady, I accept that this is your home and it's your right to stay. I wouldn't dream of trying to force your hand. All I would wish however is that you stuck to the letter of our contract regarding the repayment. Now this is taking longer and longer. If it were up to some of my comrades, they would collect on this loan double quick and you would end up losing this house to repay it. But because of my long association with your good self, this will not be the case. But I tell you it is getting harder and harder, especially with these outbursts from Mrs Marsh. They're causing a lot of ill will amongst my members.

DAPHNE. We're very grateful for your support, Mr Chakravatty.

JONES. Yes, it's very decent of you.

From round the side of the verandah appears BERTIE MARSH, *69, Anglo-Indian. He is lighting his pipe.*

BERTIE. Muriel, are you alright?

MURIEL. Couldn't be better.

CHAKRA. Ah, Mr Marsh, I was wondering when you would make an appearance. Do you know your wife has just assaulted one of my members with this garden umbrella? She almost blinded him.

BERTIE. Did she indeed! (*To* MURIEL.) Well done dear, good shot.

CHAKRA. You really shouldn't encourage her Mr Marsh. She's ill, she should be in hospital, not running around in her underclothes raving like a lunatic. They lock people up for less.

MURIEL. Bugger off!

BERTIE. Yes well they also lock people up for instigating communal violence, so you'd better be bloody careful as well.

CHAKRA. What did you say?

BERTIE. Don't act the bloody innocent with me, I saw you, stirring up that mob in the bazaar with your bloody twisted, quasi-religious theories. You ought to be ashamed of yourself man. You people are tearing this country apart.

CHAKRA. Me and my people, as you call them, are uniting this country for the first time since independence. It's time we had our say instead of having to pander to minorities.

BERTIE. My brother and many like him fought a war to stop buggers like you taking over. I for one do not intend to stand idly by and watch their sacrifice spat on, by you, or anyone else who thinks like you.

CHAKRA. I fought, Mr Marsh, for the freedom of my country from the British. What were you fighting for? Your 'special relationship' with them? Where did that leave your community when the British were kicked out? Bent over with your trousers round your ankles. How quickly you all became patriots after that.

BERTIE. How dare you stand there and accuse me of treachery, when every day you betray the principles you fought for.

DAPHNE. Ohh, not now Bertie please! We haven't even had tea yet.

CHAKRA. It's alright Miss Willows, we're all entitled to our own opinion. We live in a democracy after all. I understand your point Mr Marsh, but that was then, and this is now. We're not fascists, all we want is that the rights of Hindus are recognised in this land of Hindustan. A not unreasonable demand when you consider our numbers.

BERTIE. It is when it's at the expense of every other poor bugger!

JONES. Look why don't we all just calm down, before someone says something they may regret, mmm?

CHAKRA. Yes, let's do that. It's getting too hot for all this. Mr Marsh, come over and see us, talk to our leaders, we're not the monsters you think we are. Our doors are always open to debate. But please, in future, try to keep your wife under control, or I will be forced to involve the Municipal authorities next time. Good day.

He starts to walk away.

MURIEL. Good riddance to bad rubbish!

DAPHNE *jumps in quickly to diffuse the situation.*

DAPHNE. Might we see you at the dance next week, Mr Chakravatty?

JONES. Yes do come, it'll be lovely to see you.

CHAKRA. We shall see.

MR CHAKRAVATTY *walks off.* BERTIE *comes over and sits down.*

DAPHNE. That really was quite a stupid thing to say to him Bertie. Why do you have to goad him all the time?

BERTIE. Why do you have to appease him?

DAPHNE. It's not appeasement, I'm just trying to make life easier, so we can all live here together. It doesn't help when you fill Muriel up with these ridiculous notions. You know she's not well.

MURIEL. I'm perfectly capable of filling myself up with my own notions thank you very much Daphne.

BERTIE *smiles at* MURIEL *and pats her hand lovingly.*

DAPHNE. I know you don't want any responsibility, but the least you can do is support the person you've delegated to. Honestly Bertie, I can't carry on like this for much longer. There's the repayments of Mr Chakravatty's loan which are way behind and if you care to notice he's being bloody decent about. The dance to organise, Muriel to watch. Am I supposed to do all that and negotiate peace treaties between you and Mr Chakravatty? And there's still the problem of finding someone to replace poor Mrs Gort.

DAPHNE *starts to cry and takes out her handkerchief from her sleeve.*

MURIEL. I can look after myself, I don't need a bloody wet nurse, do I Bertie?

BERTIE. No, of course you don't my darling.

DAPHNE. I don't know why I waste my breath arguing with you both, indeed I don't. Neither of you takes the least bit of notice. Any goodwill I build with Mr Chakravatty, you just knock down. If he wants to become political, so what? Who cares? Let him, as long as he doesn't demand his money all in one go.

MURIEL. Daphne dear, why don't you go and take a little nip of something, you're becoming quite hysterical.

DAPHNE *is hurt by this reference to her drinking.*

DAPHNE. I'll take my breakfast inside. Do you want me to send Elliot out with a wrap for you?

MURIEL. No, I'll be fine. According to the doctors, I'm well past the warm wrap stage by now.

DAPHNE *walks off into the house,* MR JONES *takes the garden umbrella and puts it back in the table, opening it out. He walks over to the wall, picks up a watering can and starts to water the flowers in that area.*

BERTIE. So, how are you really feeling?

MURIEL. Well, apart from the dreadful pain in my head, and the fact that I can barely remember a thing, from one minute to the next, I'm fine. It's Daphne and all her bloody fussing that's more likely to kill me. I know she means well, but she's hardly Mother Theresa. What with her drinking and my bloody antics, we must look a right pair.

BERTIE *smiles,* MURIEL *winces as if in pain.*

MURIEL. Ohhhh, put your hand on my head and make it better.

BERTIE *starts to massage the back of* MURIEL*'s head.*

MURIEL. Mmmm, that feels so good.

BERTIE. What happened before, was it 'One of your turns'?

MURIEL *laughs out loud, clapping her hands.* BERTIE *smiles at her.*

MURIEL. Good heavens no! Just that silly old sod and his bloody ubermenschen next door . . . why she had to go and ask the old bugger to the dance is beyond me.

She closes her eyes again, and groans a little. BERTIE *puts his hands on her temples and massages them gently. He is concerned.*

BERTIE. Are you sure you're alright, would you like your pills?

MURIEL. No, no, it's nothing, just erm . . . me getting too excited.

She rides the pain for a moment, taking his hands and pressing them to her temples. She takes a deep breath and lets it out. The sound of crows can be heard.

MURIEL. Dear, oh dear. 'Those whom the gods wish to destroy, they first make mad' . . . Do you believe that?

BERTIE. Certainly not. What god would dare to destroy you?

MURIEL. I don't know, it makes you wonder though.

BERTIE. We've lived in the land of gods all our lives and never had cause to fear any of them before. So why start now?

MURIEL. I don't know, it scares me, perhaps they never really accepted us. Perhaps they were just playing tricks with us as gods do, and this is the price I have to pay.

BERTIE. Then we'll all have to pay a price eventually, but I'll be buggered if I'm going to take it lying down. Now stop being so bloody morbid.

Beat.

MURIEL. What are you going to do my love? When it happens. We should talk about it you know? While I'm still able.

BERTIE. Now come on, we'll have none of that. It's not going to happen for a long time, so let's not get ahead of ourselves.

MURIEL (*trying to get him to talk*). Bertie, please?

BERTIE. No. No, not yet, I'm not ready for that yet.

He shouts towards the house.

BERTIE. Elliot! Elliot! Where the hell are you boy! (*To* MURIEL.) We're going to get you dressed, then we'll go into town, have a wander round the cemetery, and if you're especially well behaved, we'll go on to one of those big bloody hotels and have some fun. How would you like that?

MURIEL *laughs*.

MURIEL. I should like that very much.

ELLIOT *comes onto the verandah.*

ELLIOT. Y'all wanted something?

BERTIE. Come along boy, help Missy Baba to dress.

ELLIOT *comes over to* MURIEL, *he tries to help her out of her chair.*

MURIEL. Take your hands off me, I'm not an invalid. I nearly scaled that bloody wall this morning. Sherpa Tensing couldn't have clambered up there quicker than me.

ELLIOT *looks to* BERTIE. BERTIE *gives him a nod.*

ELLIOT. Ok, Missy Baba, whatever you want.

MURIEL. And I'll get myself ready if you don't mind. I've witnessed your dress sense, Norma Jean.

ELLIOT *follows her off up to the house.* BERTIE *sits down in one of the chairs.* MR JONES *who has been watering the jasmine, puts down the watering can, comes over and sits down next to* BERTIE. *He takes out a handkerchief and wipes the back of his neck and head. Again the crows.*

JONES. Monsoon's late in coming, it always seems to be, now. (*Beat.*) Is it me, or does it get later every year? I was thinking, perhaps this year we could give the place a lick of paint. Get Elliot up on a ladder to do the high bits, shouldn't be a problem.

Pause.

BERTIE *is lost in thought.* MR JONES *looks at him. He puts his hand on* BERTIE's *and pats it.*

JONES. How are you coping old man?

Slight pause.

BERTIE. You know to tell you the truth, I don't know any more. When we found out about her illness I thought, we'll cope, we're a team, we'll handle this together. Now I feel so alone. I seem to be losing bits of her day by day. A year here, a memory there . . . things one thought you'd never forget, all just gone. It's as if a part of myself fades away as well and there's simply nothing I can do . . . even with everyone around it's just so incredibly lonely . . . I'm sorry, I'm not very good at all this. She wasn't too bad before, was she?

JONES. No, nothing we couldn't handle. Daphne's very good with her when she gets a bit much.

BERTIE. She just doesn't want to be mollycoddled, she can't bear it, never could. I know Daphne means well, but she can be so bloody infuriating at times.

JONES. It's just her way. She still thinks she's in Pondicherry, with a house full of servants and a French General in tow. It's hard for her, Bertie.

BERTIE. I know, and it's not getting any easier with Muriel.

JONES. Do we know how bad it will get?

BERTIE. What do doctors know? She shouldn't be walking around now according to them. One little sod said it was a problem 'inherent in people of mixed blood'.

JONES. What did you say to that?

BERTIE. Say? I didn't say anything. I did what any Anglo-Indian in my place would have done. I slapped his bloody face.

BERTIE *smiles at this, so does* MR JONES.

JONES. You didn't!

BERTIE. So I was in no mood for Chakravatty this morning.

JONES. You should try and ignore him.

BERTIE. I find it hard, especially when I see him in the bazaar preaching his drivel to those poor ignorant sods.

JONES. They're prepared to swallow any rubbish these fellows will feed them. I can't believe Mr Chakravatty is so involved in it all.

BERTIE. Bloody politician wallah, he knows exactly what he wants from it. Power.

JONES. Perhaps we shouldn't be so hasty in our judgement.

BERTIE. It's Muriel I'm more worried about, she gets so angry . . . it isn't good for her.

JONES. She does seem to get terribly distressed by the goings-on next door.

BERTIE. I should try and get her away from this place, if only for a while.

JONES. What about the hills? Get her out of this heat, it can't be helping her much.

BERTIE. She hates the hills, there were always too many bloody British. Put her off for life.

JONES. Perhaps a trip to Gopalpur-on-Sea would do her the world of good. I've an old friend who has a guest house there, at least I think he still has it, right on the beach, not too expensive. I'm sure he'll give you a discount if I drop him a line. He's a very nice chap, you'll like him, stout fellow, very trustworthy . . . It's such a long time since I've been. Not since my Harriet died . . . We'd go every year, even spent our honeymoon there. Personally, I'd . . . well, I'd have preferred the hills, but you know how strong-willed Harriet was. It had to be the coast for her, every year without fail. It was the waves you see Bertie, she loved the waves. She'd stand there for hours watching and listening. 'Going to Beachy Head' she called it, not that she'd ever been to Beachy Head mind, she'd only ever seen postcards of England. I think she liked the image the name conjured up. But she was there, on that sand, at Gopalpur-on-sea, she was at Beachy Head. With every wave she was there.

Pause.

BERTIE. Do you still miss her Mr Jones, even now, after all this time?

JONES. Every minute of every day I mourn her passing. I will do until the day I die. That's the day I'll take off these widow's weeds.

BERTIE. How can you have someone for so long . . . be with them, share things together . . . love them with . . . everything you have. Yet every time I see Muriel now, I feel as though she goes further and further away from me. I'm grieving for her now and she's not . . . gone anywhere yet.

JONES. Who said anything about grieving, I said I mourn her passing. I don't mope around wailing. Life's for the living, my clothes remind me of who I am and what I've lost.

From the house we hear the sound of a gramophone record playing 'J'attendrai' sung by Tino Rossi. Now and then we hear DAPHNE's reed-like voice joining in.

JONES. Oh dear, she's playing her French records. She must have been more upset than she looked.

BERTIE *stands and shouts for* ELLIOT.

BERTIE. Elliot! That mutt's been and bought her a bottle. Elliot! (*To* MR JONES.) Ohhh, ye gods! Not the French General *and* Chakravatty, not in one day. That would be more than I could bear. Elliot! Where the hell are you, you bloody dunderhead!

ELLIOT *comes running from the house quite flustered.*

BERTIE. Did you buy Miss Daphne a bottle?

ELLIOT. No Bertie sahib, she bought it herself. Now she's locked in her room singing to her French General and all. There was nothing I could do yaar.

We can hear DAPHNE *singing at the top of her voice.*

BERTIE. She can't be that sloshed, she's only been gone ten minutes or so.

ELLIOT. She bought country liquor in the bazaar. Makes you doolally damn quick man.

MURIEL *comes out from the house, now wearing an old straw hat, a dress/cardigan ensemble with a battered handbag that has seen better days.*

MURIEL. She's completely sozzled again. It's not that I mind, it's the tales of her frog bloody General I can't stand. 'Will he ever come back', she said. 'Well of course he won't you silly sod', I said. 'He had the best years of your life then buggered off back to La Belle France with not so much as an 'Au revoir mon amour'. So she burst into tears and locked herself in her room. Now can we go and eat, I'm bloody starving?

Enter VIOLET *from the gate, She is carrying a large picture of the ex-King-Emperor George Sixth.*

MURIEL. Oh for goodness sake Violet, what have you picked up now?

VIOLET. The ex-King-Emperor, he was propped up against a temple near the cemetery.

JONES. But you already have so many, where are we going to find the wall space for another one?

VIOLET. Mr Jones I couldn't just leave him on the street. A sacred cow was about to do something dreadful to his late Majesty. He looked so sad, it was as if he was asking me to help him.

BERTIE. Which is a damn sight more than he would have said to you when he was King bloody Emperor.

MURIEL. Quite right Bertie. Violet, toss the bugger out into the street where he belongs. Just like they did to us.

VIOLET. I will do nothing of the sort. The municipal author-ities have practically torn down all our statues as it is, and what have they done with them? Stuck them in a corporation park in Barrackpore, they look like a bunch of bloody refugees seeking asylum. No, there's a spot in the resident's room. He'll have pride of place at the dance.

JONES. No there isn't, you put a print there of the Gordon Highlanders at the relief of Lucknow.

VIOLET. I've always been partial to the swell of the pipes.

MURIEL. Darling it's all got to stop. We're bulging at the bloody seams with ex-imperial masters. There's barely enough room for the rest of us.

VIOLET. Then I'll find space in my own room.

BERTIE. You're already sleeping with six Viceroys, two King-Emperors . . .

JONES. Not forgetting the Queen.

MURIEL. Precisely, you can't possibly throw General Kitchener out, it'd be so unfair.

BERTIE *starts to laugh.*

VIOLET. Oh, and I saw Olivia Gibbs, she said to send you her best and that you really must call on her before they go.

MURIEL. Go where?

VIOLET. Didn't you know? She's emigrating. Going to join her sister Agnes in Australia. You remember Agnes? Lost an eye in thirty-seven at the institute dance, playing housey-housey. Left in forty-eight with an Australian sheep farmer to live in the out-back.

BERTIE. Out of the frying pan into the fire. But that was Agnes, always was two annas short of a rupee.

MURIEL. What the bloody hell does Olivia want to go and emigrate for at her age? And to Australia of all places. Isn't it full of foreigners now? Boat people and Greeks and what have you.

VIOLET. They want to spend their last days amongst their own, they get so lonely at Railway Colony. Every year fewer of our people stay. It's nearly all Indians now. Do you know, they've turned the club into a temple and what's worse, there's not a potted plant to be seen in any of the gardens, which is a personal tragedy for me, as my mother planted some hardy perennials in our bungalow before she died. One can only wonder at what fate befell them.

MURIEL. This really is bloody inconvenient. What about our whist drives. She's a deserter! If there were a war on I'd have her shot.

JONES. I hardly think it would hold up in a court-martial, and if she misses her family?

BERTIE. Muriel's right, we should be setting an example to our youngsters. We're Indians, this is our country. Christ man, if the community gets any smaller we'll be extinct.

VIOLET. Well, she told me to tell you, so it's up to you if you want to say goodbye. I shall miss her, she was always coming up with the odd knick-knack. So many packing cases she had. She can't take everything she said, so she's offered me a bas-relief of the Delhi Coronation Durbar of 1903. Oh yes, and I think we've had an answer to our advertisement. I picked it up on the way here.

She takes out a letter from her pocket and hands it to BERTIE. *He opens it and starts to read.*

JONES. Shouldn't we wait and give that to Daphne? We did make her house superintendent.

MURIEL. This is true Mr Jones, but unfortunately, as you know, our great leader is soused.

VIOLET. Oh dear, not the General again?

BERTIE. Good heavens!

MURIEL. What? What does it say?

BERTIE. Muriel, you're not going to like this one little bit.

MURIEL. Well what does it say?

BERTIE. It's from a Mrs Buller-Hughes, she says she'll take the room as it sounds perfect for her needs and is well within her budget.

MURIEL. What's wrong with that?

BERTIE. Mrs Buller-Hughes is an English woman.

MURIEL *takes the letter and starts to read it.*

BERTIE. Just there. Where it says 'A few things about myself'.

JONES. It could be quite nice, we do need to get someone in.

VIOLET. And it's not as if she's an Indian.

JONES. Really Violet, I wish you wouldn't talk like that.

VIOLET. What I mean is that there won't be a problem over the kind of things she eats. You know how fussy they are about their food.

MR JONES *doesn't quite believe her, but before he can say anything else* MURIEL *speaks.*

MURIEL. How dare she! How dare she go ahead without consulting us! How dare she say yes to allowing one of them to come and stay in this house. She's gone too bloody far this time, Bertie.

JONES. But she might be very pleasant, why don't we wait and see Mrs Marsh.

MURIEL. I'm not having no bloody English woman, Burrah mem-sahibing me again. It was bad enough when they ruled the bloody place, looking down their damn noses at us. We weren't good enough for them then, so what does she want with us now?

MURIEL *starts to walk over to the house.*

BERTIE. What are you going to do?

MURIEL. Do? I'll tell you what I'm going to do. I'm about to have one of my bloody turns!

MURIEL *heads for the house followed by* BERTIE *and* MR JONES.

Scene Two

A week later, mid-morning, still we hear the sounds of Calcutta outside. The table and chairs have been moved under the tree down stage right. ELLIOT is talking to DAPHNE, MR JONES is sat reading the paper, VIOLET is playing patience.

ELLIOT. I'm polishing the floor in the dining room for the dancing then Missy Baba came in and wanted to know what room y'all are putting Mrs Buller-Hughes in. So I said I didn't know and she called me a liar and that I looked like a chimpanzee monkey. What am I supposed to do yaar? I'm no monkey, I mean ya, I've fallen on hard times, OK. But I'm a fully trained professional cabaret artist with my own wardrobe man.

DAPHNE. Elliot, Missy Baba isn't herself at the moment and she may well say some unkind things to us all. But she doesn't mean them. She just gets confused. So we must all accept it and ignore any of the rude things she says.

VIOLET. Yes take no notice of her Elliot, you look nothing like a gorilla.

ELLIOT. It was a chimp.

VIOLET. A chimp? Oh well that's another matter, she may have a point . . .

JONES (*shutting her up*). Violet, why don't you go and get some Nimbu pani?

VIOLET. What's wrong with the boy, has he lost the use of his hands?

JONES. He's busy.

VIOLET. Have me cleaning bloody toilets like an untouchable next, I suppose.

VIOLET *goes off into the house. Mumbling to herself.*

ELLIOT. Missy Baba refuses to sleep on the same corridor as the English woman. She said she'd rather have a chimp's room than sleep near that bloody woman.

DAPHNE. Don't worry, I'll talk to Missy Baba. You just make sure the room's ready for Mrs Buller-Hughes. Now run along and sort it out.

ELLIOT *goes off towards the house and off.* MR JONES *comes over to* DAPHNE.

DAPHNE. It's just one thing after another.

JONES. Do you think Muriel really will cause any trouble?

DAPHNE. We need the money. I don't see Muriel living in one of those All India Anglo-Indian retirement homes, do you? So she'll just have to get used to the idea.

JONES. This business with Mr Chakravatty is very disturbing. Do you think he really believes all this nonsense about India for Hindus? He used to be such a nice man.

DAPHNE. He still is. It's probably just a fad he's going through. He did exactly the same thing with the yoga until he put his back out.

JONES. But what about all this martial music and the flags and slogans. It's all becoming very sinister. My friend, Mr Hussein, had all his windows smashed.

DAPHNE. I'm sure Mr Chakravatty wouldn't have had anything to do with that.

JONES. They're very powerful in Bombay now you know. They can bring the whole of Maharashtra State to a standstill at the whim of their leader.

DAPHNE. Well that's Bombay, not here. You can always rely on the Bengalis for common sense. Best of the bunch. We've had a communist government for years.

VIOLET *returns with a jug of lime water.*

VIOLET. Bloody Bolsheviks the lot of 'em. I'm not too sure how this tastes, if it's horrid we'll get the boy to make some more.

JONES. Violet, do you know anything about these people Mr Chakravatty's mixed up with?

VIOLET. Who, the buggers next door? Bad types the lot of them, bloody junglis from the bazaar. Slit your throat soon as look at you.

DAPHNE *is still not convinced.*

DAPHNE. Well I don't see Mr Chakravatty being responsible for any of the trouble. He was strictly non-violent during the fight for independence. Took quite a few beatings as well, I hear.

VIOLET. Yes, and got quite a taste for it by all accounts.

JONES. Violet, sometimes you go too far.

VIOLET. It's true, I swear, I had an uncle in the police force. He said Mr Chakravatty used to come back time after time for a thrashing. They were on first name terms by Independence Day.

JONES. That was simply part of the strategy of non-violence, not some kind of sexual deviance.

VIOLET. Please yourself but it's true.

DAPHNE. Violet, why don't you go and put some flowers in Mrs Buller-Hughes' room?

VIOLET. Yes, what a lovely thought, and perhaps I should put up a picture or a bust of a Viceroy or something, make her feel at home. What do you think?

DAPHNE *and* MR JONES *look at each other.*

JONES. Well perhaps just a small one.

VIOLET. Or I've a print of the massacre at the Ghats at Cawnpore.

DAPHNE. I think that bust of Lady Willingdon will suffice.

JONES. Yes, something a little homely. We don't want to scare her off.

VIOLET. Maybe I'll leave my copy of 'Horrors of the Indian Mutiny'. It's a damn good read, makes your hair stand on end. What the bloody natives did to our people was out-rageous. Wanton butchery, it was. My father used to read us tales from it as children. That's why I always sleep with a knife under my pillow. You never know when the buggers will get it into their heads to start it all over again.

JONES. That was in 1857.

VIOLET. Yes, well this time they won't find a member of the Wallis family asleep in their beds. Look what happened to poor Muriel in '47, well not me.

DAPHNE. Violet do be quiet!

JONES. What was this?

VIOLET. You don't know do you? Well it barely had a mention in the papers. Everyone was too busy reading about the natives killing each other. One of our girls being raped was nothing to them. They never got to the bottom of it. My Uncle was involved in the case, you know, the one who used to thrash Mr Chakravatty, so we knew everything that was going on. They did arrest someone, but there was no concrete evidence and what with the hand-over of power and all, the British weren't interested. He got off scot-free, had the right connections with the local Congress wallah.

DAPHNE. Now that's enough! I don't think Muriel will be best pleased about you washing her dirty linen in public.

VIOLET. Neither was she best pleased with you letting an English woman come and live with us. But you went ahead and did it.

DAPHNE. How many times must I explain to you people, we need money! What you and the others fail to understand is the serious predicament we're in at the moment. We're thousands of rupees in arrears. We only exist on the goodwill of Mr Chakravatty and how long that'll last I don't know. So if Mahatma bloody Gandhi came to the door asking for a room he'd get one. Never mind a sodding English woman!

Unbeknownst to DAPHNE, LYDIA BULLER-HUGHES *has just walked in behind her. She's about fifty-nine, tall, and elegantly dressed. Her hair is grey and bobbed. She carries two suitcases, which she puts down either side of her. She clears her throat, the others turn to her.*

LYDIA. Ahem . . . if the Mahatma's not taking the room, is it still available? Hello, I'm Lydia Buller-Hughes.

DAPHNE. Oh . . . erm, I'm so sorry we were erm . . .

MR JONES *walks over to her holding his hand out.*

JONES. Please ignore us, welcome, welcome to Dum Dum. I'm Mr Jones.

He shakes her hand, as DAPHNE *and* VIOLET *come over.*

DAPHNE. How do you do, I'm Daphne Willows, you wrote to me. I'm . . . erm, sort of in charge, so if you have any problems you come to me. I'm sorry, this is Violet Wallis.

LYDIA *shakes their hands.*

JONES. Is this all your luggage?

LYDIA. Crikes no, the rest is outside in the taxi.

DAPHNE. Elliot! Elliot!

DAPHNE *goes over to the house calling for* ELLIOT.

VIOLET. Elliot's our boy. Come and sit down, he'll sort out your bags.

DAPHNE. Elliot! Where are you! I'm sorry, he was here a minute ago.

JONES. You must be tired, please come and sit down.

VIOLET. Did you travel far?

LYDIA. From Assam.

VIOLET. How lovely, and were your people in tea?

LYDIA *is slightly amused at this comment.*

LYDIA. Yes, as a matter of fact my husband was, before he retired.

VIOLET. Yes I thought so.

DAPHNE. Elliot! Where's that damn boy got to?

JONES. Well we're quite a small family here, just us three, and Bertie and Muriel.

DAPHNE. Elliot!

VIOLET. And Elliot. He's also our cook. We used to have a separate cook as well, but he was an untouchable and was done to death in the last riots. Probably by the people next door we think . . . they're quite extreme, do anything to annoy us.

JONES. Oh Violet please, I do apologise Mrs Buller-Hughes but Violet does tend to exaggerate. We had to let the cook go for financial reasons.

VIOLET. But he's never been seen since. Not a trace.

She draws her finger across her neck and makes a cutting sound. ELLIOT *appears on the verandah.*

ELLIOT. Y'all want something?

DAPHNE. Elliot, Mrs Buller-Hughes has arrived, could you go out to the taxi and get her bags. And when you've done that, bring out some more Nimbu-pani. I'm sorry Violet but this is quite undrinkable. (*She turns to* LYDIA.) You would like some? Or we can get you something else?

LYDIA. No, that would be lovely.

JONES. Would you like something to eat? We've had lunch, but we could have Elliot rustle something up for you? It's no bother.

LYDIA. No thanks, I ate on the train.

VIOLET. Oh you brave thing, you must have been starving, to eat that greasy food. I can't touch it myself. Gives me the trots something chronic I tell you.

MR JONES *is trying to get rid of* VIOLET.

JONES. Why don't you go and see if Bertie and Muriel are at the cemetery?

DAPHNE. Would you like to see your room, it's all ready for you?

LYDIA. I'll just catch my breath a moment if you don't mind.

DAPHNE. Yes of course, you must be tired.

Pause. Silence.

JONES. No monsoon yet. Gets later every year.

VIOLET. Sends people doolally this kind of heat does. Bound to be trouble in the bazaar. Last year Mr Roy, who sells tiffin boxes, made a perfectly innocent comment about oral hygiene. Well, they burnt all his hair off, terrible, looked like a singed pig. I . . .

MR JONES *cut her off.*

JONES. Not doing my flowers any good either.

LYDIA *is still looking at* VIOLET *after her odd story. Then turns to* MR JONES.

JONES. The heat.

LYDIA. No, it's erm, it's a lovely garden, Mr Jones.

VIOLET. He's very gifted with the green fingers. Grows anything he can.

ELLIOT *staggers through with the cases from outside.*

DAPHNE. Hurry with those drinks Elliot.

LYDIA. It's delightful Mr Jones.

JONES. Thank you, my wife laid it out and I've muddled along with it ever since. But do feel free to muck in if you wish.

LYDIA. Thank you, I'd like to.

DAPHNE. It's our oasis isn't it Mr Jones.

VIOLET. Do you like statues?

LYDIA. I beg your pardon?

VIOLET. Well busts really. I can't quite persuade the others to let me have anything bigger than a head. There isn't the space, well not in my room anyway. If you see anything you like you're quite welcome to have it in your room. I've a varied collection of Generals, Viceroys, Kings and Queens, so do help yourself. Though Field Marshal Lord Roberts's can't be removed from the games room, we use him for quoits. Disrespectful to the victor of Kandahar I know, but part of the bargain I had to make to keep him here.

LYDIA. Thank you Violet, I shall think about it.

VIOLET. Have you read 'Horrors of the Mutiny'?

DAPHNE *quickly interjects.*

DAPHNE. How many years have you been in India?

LYDIA. Came out in thirty-seven. Been back to England once, last year when my husband died. Couldn't stick it, awful place, didn't recognise a thing, and that dreadful Thatcher woman, worse kind of box-wallah you could meet. Came back here double quick, I can tell you.

VIOLET. You went to England and came back here? My god you're barking bloody mad, woman!

DAPHNE *and* MR JONES *are shocked but* LYDIA *finds it very amusing.*

JONES. Violet, don't be so rude!

LYDIA. It's alright, Mr Jones.

VIOLET. But she came back to live here!

LYDIA. India's my home, I've lived more of my life here than I have in England.

VIOLET. Still, it's a bit bloody rum if you ask me. If I'd have had the money in forty-seven I'd have been off like a shot. Wouldn't have thought twice about leaving the place. I ended up looking after some old Colonel's wife who stayed on, a ladies' companion I was supposed to be, nothing but a bloody skivvy. She died in 1975, leaving me one gold sovereign, a gilt framed portrait of Madam Blavatsky and a year's membership to the Theosophical Society. They contact the dead you know. It's a good job I never contacted that old skinflint 'cause I'd have given her a piece of my bloody mind.

Enter from the gate, MURIEL, *she has in her hands the remnants of posters she has been tearing off walls. She has been running and looks dishevelled; strands of hair cover her face. She has worked herself up into a state.*

MURIEL. Damn them! Damn them all to hell! Bertie! Where are you? Bertie! You! Yes you!

She points to DAPHNE *but does not take in* LYDIA.

MURIEL. All this is your doing, I'm holding you personally responsible for this. If you hadn't told him when the dance was he wouldn't have done this.

DAPHNE. Who's done what? What am I supposed to have done now?

MURIEL. Look at this, read it, and tell me you're not responsible. Here Mr Jones, see if I'm not right.

MURIEL *hands over one of the torn posters to* DAPHNE. *She gives one to* MR JONES *as well.*

JONES. Why don't you come and sit down?

VIOLET. What is it Muriel, what's wrong?

MURIEL. Wrong? I'll tell you what's wrong. Captain bloody Bligh here only invited Chakravatty to the dance. Now he's decided to hold a rally on the same night. The same night! All because this stupid bugger invited him. He's doing it to spite us.

DAPHNE. I don't think this has got anything to do with me inviting him. It's pure coincidence.

MURIEL. Whose fault is it then? Mine? Bertie's? It's yours, you stupid woman! We didn't want him here but you wouldn't listen, would you. You just went ahead and asked him anyway.

JONES. Muriel, please, we have a guest.

MURIEL. Sod the guest! I didn't ask her to come.

MURIEL *is steadily becoming more and more manic which is symptomatic of her condition. She touches the side of her head for a moment as if in pain.*

JONES. Are you all right Mrs Marsh, shall I go and get Bertie?

MURIEL. Stay there! You leave Bertie alone!

DAPHNE goes towards her and tries to calm her down.

JONES. I think we really should get the doctor.

DAPHNE. Why don't we go inside and talk about this, mm?

MURIEL. You have no idea the bloodshed these people would
cause if they ever got into power, do you? I mean do you
care, have you ever stopped to think? You know I . . .
I wonder, at you sometimes, truly I do. You're all of you
pitiful, look at yourselves, pretending, hiding in this bloody
house with your heads in the sand. I know you laugh at me
behind my back, you don't think I know, do you? Well I'm
not that ill yet that I can't see who my real friends are. You
make me sick the lot of you; you're spineless, just like those
bastards next door. So next time...

*She suddenly drops to the ground and goes into a fit.
Her body is rigid but is twitching rapidly. VIOLET screams
and jumps out of the way behind a chair for protection.
DAPHNE rushes over to MURIEL followed by MR JONES.*

VIOLET. Look at her! What's wrong with her?

DAPHNE. My god Mr Jones, I don't know what to do, I've
never seen her like this!

JONES. I'll call for the doctor.

*LYDIA quickly rushes over to MURIEL and starts to
straighten her body, she then reaches into MURIEL's mouth
and tries to keep the tongue from rolling back and choking
her.*

LYDIA. Mr Jones, can I have your pen please!

*She takes the pen and slips it across MURIEL's mouth to
stop her biting down on her tongue.*

JONES. Is she going to be alright?

LYDIA. I think so, has this happened before?

DAPHNE. No, never, but she's very ill, a brain tumour.

LYDIA. Then you'd better send for the doctor quickly.

MR JONES *rushes off into the house.*

JONES. Elliot! Elliot!

VIOLET. She might be rabid, check for froth!

DAPHNE. Violet, go and get a blanket.

VIOLET. I mean, why's she doing that awful shaking?

LYDIA. She'll be fine Violet, she's having a fit, but we really do need a pillow for her head.

VIOLET. Yes, right of course, I'll get my own.

She runs off into the house.

DAPHNE. Should we give her a brandy or something?

LYDIA. Better not, best wait for the doctor, though maybe a little water, I'm not sure.

DAPHNE. I'll go and get some.

She goes off into the house. MURIEL *stops shaking and begins to come round.* LYDIA *takes the pen from her mouth.*

MURIEL. Am I dead?

LYDIA. Not quite, you had a fit.

MURIEL. Get me up.

LYDIA. I think it would be better if you just lay still a while.

MURIEL. Sod that. If I'm going to die, I'll die on me feet. Not on the ground like a beggar.

LYDIA *helps her into a chair.*

MURIEL. Did I get myself into a bit of a state?

LYDIA. You did a bit.

MURIEL. Thought so, felt it coming. Didn't quite expect this though. I'm dying, they did tell you that, didn't they? Don't go getting it into your head that you've saved me, you've just postponed the inevitable. It was you who stuck that Mont Blanc in my mouth?

LYDIA. Yes, it's Mr Jones'; he's gone to fetch the doctor. I'm
    Lydia Buller-Hughes.

MURIEL. Just my luck. Life saved by a bloody English
    woman!

Interval.

36

ACT TWO

Scene One

It's late afternoon, the day before the dance. LYDIA
BULLER-HUGHES *stands on some stepladders pinning up
paper lanterns, she is helped by* ELLIOT. *The garden is
looking more festive now, with little flags of India and Great
Britain hanging up. A portrait of the present Queen Elizabeth
and her family hangs above the steps flanked by two little
Union Jacks. In the distance, we can hear the constant noise
of Indian street life: car horns, hawkers selling their wares,
the sound of crows.* VIOLET *comes out onto the verandah,
she's getting ready to go out.*

VIOLET. Ohhh, this is very lovely. You're doing a wonderful
  job, Lydia. Elliot, did Mr and Mrs Marsh say where they
  were going?

  *We hear a beggar over by the gate crying out in the usual
  deep grating sound they have.* VIOLET *is annoyed at this.
  She walks over to the gate but not too close.*

  What is it? What do you want? (*To* LYDIA.) These buggers
  come back each week, it's Bertie and Muriel, they spoil
  them. (*Back to the beggar.*) The sahib isn't here, he's out,
  bazaar jaata hun. Burrah memsahib is not here either, shoo,
  shoo, away, jao! Jao!

  LYDIA *takes some change from her pocket.*

LYDIA. Here Elliot, run and give him this.

  ELLIOT *takes the money and runs out of the gate after the
  beggar.*

VIOLET. You shouldn't encourage them you know.

  ELLIOT *takes out a letter.*

ELLIOT. Mrs Wallis, your letter is here.

She gestures him to hand it over.

VIOLET. Give it here then boy, come on, don't take all day about it.

She takes the letter and without a second thought, tears it in half. She tosses it to ELLIOT.

VIOLET. Dustbin with it. Right I'm off, there's a chicken in the back,we'll have a Country-Captain for supper.

VIOLET *leaves.* LYDIA *looks to* ELLIOT *for some explanation.*

LYDIA. What on earth was all that about?

ELLIOT. Every month Violet receives a letter from her daughter Millicent. She won't speak to her, has nothing to do with her, so she tears them up without reading them.

LYDIA. But why, what happened?

ELLIOT. Millicent went native and ran off with a religious mendicant from Wankaner. Violet never spoke to her again. 'Taking up religion is one thing' she said 'But running off with a naked fakir is just not the done thing'.

LYDIA. Oh, I see.

ELLIOT *is now in his gossipy stride.*

ELLIOT. The second husband was the father of Millicent, Cuthbert Jenkins. He was a crooner with the Bombay Ragtime Rascals. He died of cholera just after the war, though she's still in regular communication with him through the theosophical society . . . He favours reconciliation by all accounts, but Violet says 'he's just as blithering an idiot dead, as he was alive' . . . Don't worry madame, Daphne always drops Millicent a little note to say her mother's doing well.

LYDIA. That's very sad, she should try and patch things up, doesn't do to let things go on like that.

LYDIA *stands back and looks at her handiwork.*

There, how's that looking? Are they straight?

ELLIOT. They look fantastic yaar. Y'all want some water now?

LYDIA. Mmm, please. Are you sure they look level? They look a little crooked to me.

ELLIOT. Madame your bunting looks great. The garden will look fantastic for the dance.

LYDIA. I was always quite a dab hand at this. Used to help out with amateur theatricals at the club. Operas and musicals, I bet you didn't think I was a singer did you? Do you know any Gilbert and Sullivan? (*She starts to hum.*) 'Three little maids from school are we, etc, etc'.

LYDIA *does a bit from the operetta,* ELLIOT *looks on curiously. He applauds at the end, not quite knowing when that is.*

ELLIOT. Madam, that was great yaar, you have a lovely voice. I bet you could have been a star.

LYDIA. Oh stop trying to flatter me. They were club theatricals. Gilbert and Sullivan during the hot season and The Desert Song at Christmas.

ELLIOT. You know, I used to sing as well.

LYDIA. Then it's your turn to entertain me.

ELLIOT. Nooo, yaar I'm too shy.

LYDIA. Oh come along Elliot, I've just made a fool of myself. Come on, there's no one around.

ELLIOT. Ok, then.

ELLIOT *takes up a Marilyn Monroe stance.*

ELLIOT. 'A kiss on the hand might be quite continental, but diamonds are a girl's best friend etc, etc'.

LYDIA *stands there in shock.*

LYDIA. Elliot, that's wonderful, do you know any more?

ELLIOT. Of course, I was a professional cabaret artist. I did Marilyn Monroe and Hindi film heroines. Very high class, not cheap, never did bars, only hotels with legitimate cabaret lounges.

LYDIA. You didn't? Oh Elliot, how exciting. Show me, do another for me.

ELLIOT. Nooo, yaar, I'm retired.

LYDIA. But why? That was wonderful.

ELLIOT. The whole business got so seedy an' all. No one cared about character, all they wanted was flesh and instant thrills. Make it shocking and everyone flocks to see it. All my ladies were spot on you know? The hours I'd spent in cinemas getting them right. All the way down to the costumes, well, you've seen yourself, fine detail. Now all you get are these Johnnies in a wet bathing suit and a bucket of water. And they call it show business. I gave it up. There was just no call for Marilyn Monroe any more.

LYDIA. Perhaps you should have changed your act, you know you're very talented, you sound just like her.

ELLIOT. Yaa, I tried, but it just wasn't working. The magic wasn't there any more. All they wanted was for me to soak myself down and take my clothes off. It all ended when they asked for my Dimple, you know Dimple Kapadia? Big Bombay film star. Starred in 'Bobby.' My all-time favourite film. I thought things were looking up, tastes had changed, the audience had come to their senses at last. So I gave them my Dimple and half way through my first number they threw a bucket of water over me. Oh yes, they wanted Dimple, but they wanted her wet. So my career in show business ended in a wet puddle in a seedy club full of leering men.

LYDIA. Oh Elliot I am sorry, it must have been awful for you, all that hard work.

ELLIOT. I've never worn her costume again . . . (*Pause.*) It shrank.

LYDIA. Well the world of entertainment is very fickle Elliot, you're probably better off out of it. Especially that side of the business. No, you made the right career move becoming a cook.

ELLIOT. No I didn't, not straight away anyway. I spent six months as a male prostitute. Just 'til I found my feet so to speak.

LYDIA *looks shocked.*

ELLIOT. It wasn't new to me, I'd done it as a young boy. Being a professional cabaret artist had taken me away from that life. Now it was all gone and I had to live. That's why my characters were always so good. I'd spent years in dark cinemas watching those glorious films, while sweaty men smelling of cheap sandlewood soap fumbled around in my flies . . . I was quite fetching when I was younger.

LYDIA. Oh Elliot, you don't have to tell me any of this.

ELLIOT. I'm not ashamed, I survived my childhood, many didn't. British genes you see, stiff upper lip, make do with what you've got an' all.

LYDIA. So when did you end up here?

ELLIOT. Five years or so ago. It was Bertie; I met him one day in South Parks cemetery.

LYDIA *gives* ELLIOT *a quizzical look.* ELLIOT *laughs out loud.*

LYDIA. He wasn't . . .

ELLIOT. No yaar, it was nothing like that.

LYDIA. Well of course not, but one hears such horror stories of what goes on in South Parks.

ELLIOT. Well, he wasn't but I was. I was living there. On the grave of Charlotte Hickey, wife of the famous diary writer. Not that I knew who she was, or I'd have had more respect. It was Bertie who told me. He'd come on a visit. That's what they do, the others, when they get bored, they wander round the cemeteries visiting famous dead English people. Anyway, he came to visit Charlotte and found me at it with a Johnnie I'd met on Lower Circular Road. He was furious.

LYDIA *can't help but laugh at him.* ELLIOT *joins in.*

ELLIOT. It's true yaar! Though he was more shocked to see that an Anglo-Indian had let down his community, than with what he saw the Johnny doing to me on the grave of the wife of an English institution.

Enter from the front gate MR CHAKRAVATTY, *huffing and puffing as usual. He is dressed in a white dhoti and long shirt. He carries an open umbrella to protect him from the heat of the sun. In his other hand he carries his briefcase.* ELLIOT *sees him and whispers to* LYDIA.

ELLIOT. Madam, this man, be careful, he's not a nice man.

ELLIOT *assumes a deferential demeanour and goes over to him.*

CHAKRA. Fetch Miss Daphne, and some cold water. Quickly boy, quickly.

He goes toward LYDIA *with outstretched hand as* ELLIOT *runs off into the house.*

CHAKRA. I'm sorry madam, I don't think we've had the pleasure, Pershotum Chakravatty, advocate. And you are?

LYDIA. Lydia Buller-Hughes, I'm a new resident here.

CHAKRAVATTY *is taken aback for a minute.*

CHAKRA. A new resident, you mean you'll be replacing Mrs Gort, here permanently?

LYDIA. Yes.

CHAKRA. How delightful, Miss Willows did say she was looking for a new resident. How lovely to have you here. I'm your neighbour, no doubt you've heard of me by now, but you mustn't believe everything people say. I'm just next door, do feel free to call on us, our door is always open. It's not quite as comfortable as this, but it meets our needs.

LYDIA. Ahh, so it was your people with all the drums and the shouting this morning?

CHAKRA. Did we disturb you? Please accept my apologies, you see, we're practising for the arrival of a visiting leader from Mumbai.

LYDIA. Bombay, yes I know, I've seen one of your posters, sounds very interesting . . .

CHAKRA. Then you must come. Everyone is welcome.

LYDIA. I'm afraid I'm otherwise engaged that night.

CHAKRA. What a pity, he's a very interesting speaker, truly fascinating. He knows instantly where to put his finger on the problems, which unfortunately plague our country. One day, god willing, he will make a great P.M.

LYDIA. He seems to attract a lot of controversy Mr Chakravatty.

CHAKRA. In what way Mrs Buller-Hughes?

LYDIA. Well I read in an interview with him recently in one of the papers, I can't remember which, that he was a great admirer of Adolf Hitler.

Pause.

CHAKRA. Goodness no, he was misquoted. What he actually meant was that he was a great admirer of Adolf Hitler's painting.

LYDIA. Oh I see.

CHAKRA. Indeed, yes, it is a little known fact that Hitler was also a very fine draughtsman.

LYDIA. I didn't know. Then again I suppose one wouldn't. Swamped, as we were, by his many other talents.

CHAKRAVATTY *looks around at the decorations.*

CHAKRA. Look at this place, what a transformation, I must say the garden is looking splendid for the dance. You have to hand it to Mr Jones, he certainly knows his way around a garden. It was in such a terrible state, the whole house had gone to seed. What a pity the garden will have to go.

LYDIA. I'm sorry Mr Chakravatty I don't understand, go where exactly?

CHAKRA. Well I was going to tell everyone together but I suppose as we're both here you can be the first to know. (*He*

pumps himself up with pride.) My members and I have
discovered that our Lord Krishna tumbled across some
rocks and from this spot grew a tree in this very garden or
where this garden now stands. So we have to reclaim it, it is
sacred to us, and we intend to build a Temple in celebration
of the event.

Beat.

LYDIA. Of your Lord Krishna stubbing his foot on a boulder?
Well I'm no geological expert Mr Chakravatty, but it does
seem much rockier on your side of the fence. Perhaps he
stubbed it there.

CHAKRA. No madam, it was here, this is the place it
happened. Thousands will come on pilgrimage to see this
spot.

LYDIA. If you don't mind me saying so, Mr Chakravatty, I just
think it's all rather rude. You can't expect people to just
pack up and go because you've decided that something's
holy and sacred to you, I mean where does it end?

CHAKRA. I'm sorry madam, I'm letting my excitement run
away with me and we've only just met. Please forgive me.
But you must understand that these are exciting times for
us, we're discovering an identity, which has been squashed
for hundreds of years. This garden is part of that identity.

*Enter DAPHNE with ELLIOT behind carrying a glass of
water. ELLIOT goes over to MR CHAKRAVATTY and
gives it to him. MR CHAKRAVATTY takes a sip and
places the glass on the table amid the bunting.*

DAPHNE. Ah, I see you two have met.

CHAKRA. Indeed, Mrs Buller-Hughes and I were discussing
Indian history.

LYDIA. Yes, and Mr Chakravatty was telling me about Adolf
Hitler. Did you know he was a painter?

DAPHNE. Erm, no I don't think I did. Mr Chakravatty I'm
afraid you're a bit early, the others aren't here yet.

LYDIA *carries on with the bunting but also keeps a wary eye on* CHAKRAVATTY.

CHAKRA. No matter, no matter, it's nothing to trouble their heads with. Just mundane paper work.

DAPHNE. Perhaps we could have some tea.

CHAKRA. That won't be necessary, this water will be fine, so if we could just get on with this.

DAPHNE. But the others should be here really.

CHAKRA. The reason I requested everyone to be here was because I wanted to tell you about the garden.

DAPHNE. What about it?

LYDIA. Apparently Lord Krishna stubbed his toe on a rock here several thousand years ago and now Mr Chakravatty wants to turn it into a shrine.

He opens his briefcase, takes some papers out and lays them on the table with the bunting. LYDIA *takes note of this.*

DAPHNE. But that's ridiculous! You can't possibly expect us to hand over the garden because you suspect one of your deity's tripped over his sandal in it, god knows how many years ago. No, I'm sorry, I can't do that. I won't do it.

CHAKRA. All I need is your signature on some papers. I think we can dispense with your version of Indian theology.

DAPHNE. I don't wish to be a nuisance Mr Chakravatty, but I think that before I sign any papers, we should wait for the other residents. I'm quite sure they'll all have something to say about this.

CHAKRA. Miss Willows, there is no alternative, to have this shrine would bring pleasure to thousands. Will you be the one to deny them that joy?

DAPHNE. But Mr Chakravatty, you know how much this garden means to us, I can't sign it away just like that.

CHAKRA. I had hoped, Miss Willows that this situation might be resolved amicably, but I see your stubbornness is blinding you to the fact that there is still a great deal of money owing to me. Now my suggestion to you is that you sign over the garden to me and I will wipe the slate clean. The only other alternative is a long drawn-out court case where you could be forced to sell off the whole property to pay off your debts. One further condition is that you will have to resolve the problem of Mr and Mrs Marsh.

DAPHNE. What do you mean by that?

CHAKRA. I'm afraid they may have to find alternative lodgings. My members and I feel they would not be suited to these holy environs.

DAPHNE. But Mr Chakravatty, you promised.

CHAKRA. There was nothing I could do Miss Willows, I warned you so many times to control these people. But now it's gone too far. Do you know they stood up in the bazaar and accused myself and my members of being corrupt and divisive. Now the decision has been made, all I need is a signature for my lawyers on these papers, nothing more.

DAPHNE. Does it have to be signed now, today? I mean, will I get a chance to look it over?

CHAKRA. Yes, today, my own lawyer has to hand over the papers to the bank. I could do it myself but it wouldn't be ethical under the circumstances, being an interested party you see.

DAPHNE *seems to be ready to back down.*

DAPHNE. But if you could only give them another chance. Couldn't you speak again to your party members?

CHAKRA. Believe me, I have begged them on my own knees.

CHAKRAVATTY *starts to take out his pen to offer to* DAPHNE.

CHAKRA. Here allow me.

LYDIA. Let me move this bunting for you . . . Oh!

*With a flourish she whips up the bunting from the table
upsetting the tumbler of water and soaking the documents
and* CHAKRAVATTY. *She instantly starts to mop them
with the bunting, which disintegrates and starts to turn the
documents into a similar coloured mush.* CHAKRAVATTY
looks mortified and tries to salvage them.

CHAKRA. My god woman, what have you done!

LYDIA. Oh, how stupid of me! I'm so sorry Mr Chakravatty,
I'm so clumsy . . .

CHAKRAVATTY *is trying to shake out the papers.*

DAPHNE. Maybe if you laid them out in the sun?

CHAKRA. No, no, they're ruined, useless now, they'll have to
be redone. This alters nothing Miss Willows, you will still
have to make a decision over the garden.

LYDIA. I'm so so sorry Mr Chakravatty, it was entirely my
fault.

ELLIOT. It's cheap tissue paper madam, it just falls apart an'
all, I used it on some of my costumes.

DAPHNE. Yes, don't worry Lydia, we can always make some
more bunting.

CHAKRA. Never mind the damn bunting, look at my papers!

Enter from the front gate VIOLET. *She seems to be in a bit
of a flap.*

VIOLET. Oh Mr Chakravatty, thank god you're here! You have
influence with the municipal authorities, don't you?

CHAKRA. What? What are you going on about woman?
Please don't bother me now Mrs Wallis, I am in no mood
for your antics.

VIOLET. You're in charge of the council or something, aren't
you?

CHAKRA (*irritated*). Well some of my comrades sit on the
council, if that's what you mean.

VIOLET. Then you must rally their support to my aid. I've just come from the Maidan where I heard a couple of corporation wallahs discussing the removal of the statue of Lord Mayo.

CHAKRA. What the blazes are you talking about woman! Miss Willows, do all your residents belong in an insane asylum!

DAPHNE. Oh really Violet, you're taking this hobby of yours too far now. Mr Chakravatty has far more important things to do than to waste his time with some silly old statue.

VIOLET. This is part of our heritage you're talking about. Surely you understand, Mr Chakravatty?

CHAKRA. Miss Wallis, for the last time . . .

LYDIA. Now remind me Violet, which one was he?

VIOLET *quotes from the statue.*

VIOLET. 'To the honourable and beloved memory of Richard Southwell, 6th Earl of Mayo, Humane, Courteous, Resolute and Enlightened. Struck down in the midst of a Patriotic and Beneficent career on the 18th February 1872 by the treacherous hand of an assassin. The people of India, mourning and indignant, raise this statue.'

LYDIA. Oh I remember him, Stabbed by a Pathan in the Andamans.

MR CHAKRAVATTY *manages to hold his temper; his day is not going according to plan.*

CHAKRA. Fortunately we 'Indians' are no longer mourning or indignant to the political assassination of an oppressor. And since we have been independent from the British for 35 years, I think it is high time that he was knocked off his perch. I'm sorry, there is nothing I can do, or wish to do. It's in the hands of the municipal authorities.

VIOLET. Then like Kim, I will 'sit in defiance of municipal orders, astride the gun Zam-Zamah'.

CHAKRA. Ahh, Kipling, a man with an observant eye for all things Indian, the sounds, the smells, the foibles of a nation, but too bloody sentimental and a rabid colonialist to boot. And from what I've read recently, of dubious sexuality.

LYDIA. Kitchener and Kipling! Is nothing sacred?

VIOLET. Why now, after all these years, embark on yet another round of vandalism against imperial statuary? What little vestige of faith I have left in this democracy, steadily recedes with every act of post-colonial hooliganism.

CHAKRAVATTY *starts to pack his briefcase.*

CHAKRA. Well I'm sorry you feel that way Mrs Wallis, but you must face the fact, it is going to happen. I myself have the honour to be on the committee to decide who shall replace him. Perhaps you have some suggestions of your own; I would be very interested in hearing them. We may even replace the statue of Gandhi as well. The youth of our country should be seeing positive images of a stronger Hindustan, a martial Hindustan. One that will stand up against all her enemies, both foreign and domestic. Miss Willows, I will return as soon as the new papers have been drawn up. I hope you will have made a sensible decision by then. Good-day ladies.

He exits through the front gate.

VIOLET. Should have done what my father suggested in '36. Put all these freedom fighter Johnnies up against a bloody wall and shot 'em. Especially his sort.

Enter BERTIE, MURIEL and MR JONES. MURIEL has her arms linked in theirs. They come over and sit under the umbrella.

MURIEL. Chakravatty seemed in a bit of a hurry, I thought he was coming to our meeting.

BERTIE. Isn't his party leader coming from Bombay next week? Thought he'd be happy with that.

MURIEL. Surely you mean Mumbai? Elliot, bring some cold water.

ELLIOT *goes off to fetch water.*

BERTIE. I bloody well mean Bombay.

MURIEL *takes note of* DAPHNE, VIOLET, *and* LYDIA.

MURIEL. And what's the matter with you three?

JONES. Now Muriel, you said you were going to behave today.

MURIEL. Bonjour Daphne, comment ça va?

DAPHNE *ignores her.*

MURIEL. Oh for god's sake Daphne, say something. Even if it's just to tell us what that dreary little man wanted.

DAPHNE *sits, she's tired.*

DAPHNE. He wanted me to sign some papers. I told him I couldn't sign anything until I'd spoken to all of you. I'm afraid he's going to take the garden and there's really nothing we can do.

BERTIE. No!

JONES. But this is my wife's garden, she made it.

BERTIE. What about the dances? We won't be able to hold them any more if he takes the garden.

DAPHNE. Well, it seems Lord Krishna danced here first.

JONES. What?

DAPHNE. They've decided this is a holy site, and he's calling in his debt.

BERTIE. What is it with these robbing bastards! Whenever they want to get their hands on anything, they just march in and claim it's sacred.

MURIEL. Over my dead body he'll get it.

VIOLET. Well, Muriel, that may well be, I mean you're not very well are you?

JONES. Violet! Was that necessary?

VIOLET. But it's true. She nearly rattled herself to death last week. If it hadn't been for Mrs Buller-Hughes' quick thinking and your biro, she'd have been a bloody gonner!

MURIEL. Thank you, Violet. I'm glad you take such an interest in my health.

BERTIE. The conniving buggers!

MURIEL. Some bloody superintendent you turned out to be! You couldn't run a sodding monkey house. Should have bloody known you'd be too soft on him.

DAPHNE. You brought this down on us Muriel, you and Bertie with your constant attacks on him. Why couldn't you just leave him alone! Do you think he's going to stop at the garden? Well do you? We'll be lucky if we have a bloody roof over our heads by the end of the year!

MURIEL. Why don't you just come out and say it? If Bertie and I left, Mr Chakravatty may look a good deal more kindly at you lot.

DAPHNE. Yes, you're right, he would, and you know something? At this moment in time, I wish you would go because I'm fed up with your self-indulgent attitude. You're dying Muriel and I'm sorry for that, but sometimes I just wish you'd get on and do it and leave the rest of us in peace!

MURIEL. At last we hear the truth.

JONES. You're being very silly now Muriel, none of us would dream of asking either of you to leave.

MURIEL. I wouldn't be so sure of your troops, Mr Jones.

VIOLET. I know we don't always see eye to eye on things Muriel, but I won't see one of my people out on the street. Especially since all this trouble's been caused by a bloody native.

MURIEL. Well thank you both for the support, but I will not be going anywhere, so if he wants to turn me out, let the bugger come and do it himself.

LYDIA. Look, no one's talking about throwing anyone out. I've an old friend, he's a retired lawyer, I'll speak to him, We should call Mr Chakravatty's bluff and go to court.

MURIEL. Christ, where have you been living for the last 35 years you stupid woman?

BERTIE *and the others can see* MURIEL *beginning to rave. As* MURIEL's *speech begins, the light reaches 'golden time' just before the dusk.*

BERTIE. Muriel, stop it!

MURIEL. No, I'm interested in what the bloody memsahib has to say, after all she's English! And we've great respect for the English. We're the same aren't we? Apart from a little nigger blood, that is. This is India dear in the '80's, any sense of fair play went with the Raj, not that there was that much around when it was still here. Not for the likes of us anyway. The place is corrupt as hell, the only justice you get is what you can pay for. That is exactly what Chakravatty and his mob know.

LYDIA. Not everyone is corrupt.

MURIEL. What do you care? Why should you be concerned with what happens to us? It didn't bother you in '47, you came out smelling of roses, everything packed and parcelled away. Pity the bloody natives spoiled it by killing each other. Still, no one harmed eh? What about us? Did you not think anything would happen to your half-bred bastards when you left?

DAPHNE. Muriel, you'll stop this right now! You're being ridiculous! Bertie, for god's sake do something!

BERTIE. Please dear.

MURIEL. I'll tell you who's bloody ridiculous, you are. The way you harp on about your life in Pondicherry, that's ridiculous. A tart, a whore that's all you were. To a Frenchman, not even a Free Frenchman, you had to go and choose a bloody Vichy Nazi. The pick of Pondicherry and she picks the only bloody Nazi of the bunch. I don't know if I should laugh at you or pity you. Did you really think he was going to take you with him or were you naive enough to think he was going to send for you? I'll tell you one thing, you must have been completely bloody doolally to

believe he was in love with you in the first place, you
pathetic bitch!

DAPHNE *does not say anything. But slowly her body
begins to rack with sobs and she drops to the verandah
steps in floods of tears.* MURIEL *has turned into a vicious
rabid dog again.*

MURIEL. Oh get up, get up, you drunken old sot, we've seen
it all before. Your crocodile tears fool nobody. You're lucky
it's not you packing your bloody bags, think of that eh,
what would you do then, mmm? Where would you go?
Everybody knows about you dear. Running off like some
painted whore with your Frenchman. Your mother died of
the shame and you, you came creeping back with your tail
between your legs.

ELLIOT. Please Missy Baba!

MURIEL. You can shut your mouth as well, you disease-ridden
tart. Or you'll find yourself on the streets with her. My god,
what a pair of whores you'll make; you wouldn't get fifty
rupees for the two of you, and they'd have to be desperate
to offer that!

BERTIE *grabs her and pulls her to him. She doesn't seem
to recognise him at first.*

BERTIE. Stop it! Just stop it Muriel! You've gone too far this
time, I won't allow you to go on saying any more of this
vileness . . .   What's happened to you? I don't recognise you
when you behave like this.

BERTIE *sees that her mind is somewhere else.*

Oh my love, don't be like this, I don't know you. I don't
like it, it's not you. Come back to me, listen to me, it's
Bertie.

MURIEL *just stares at him, she is trying to remember.*
LYDIA *goes over to comfort* DAPHNE, ELLIOT *goes into
the house followed by* VIOLET. MR JONES *goes over to
the wall and starts to pick the jasmine flowers. Silence, no
one knows what to say.* BERTIE *holds* MURIEL *to his chest
hugging her tightly. He has tears in his eyes.*

MURIEL. Bertie . . . Bertie, what's happened?

BERTIE. Hello, hello, my love, you came back then?

MURIEL. Was it one of my turns?

BERTIE. Yes. But you're alright now, you came back to me.

MURIEL. Did I do that awful shaking?

BERTIE. No, no nothing like that, you just got a bit angry, but everything's fine now.

MURIEL *buries her head in* BERTIE's *chest, she holds onto him as if she is trying to keep hold of life.*

MURIEL. Oh Bertie, hold me, don't let me go. Promise never to let go of me. It's such a dark place and I'm so scared. I don't know what happens or where I go and it gets harder and harder each time to get back to you.

BERTIE. Hush . . . shh . . . shh. There's no need to be afraid, I'll always be here waiting for you . . . Why . . . you, you just go to Beachy Head on a visit.

MURIEL *smiles and gives a little giggle.*

MURIEL. Beachy Head? . . . Oh Bertie, what are you bloody talking about, you do make me laugh.(*She giggles.*)

As she does, she notices that BERTIE *has tears in his eyes. She gently wipes away a tear from his cheek.*

MURIEL. But I like that. Beachy Head . . . Yes, that's where I'll go.

She does not see BERTIE *look across to* MR JONES. MR JONES *looks back at* BERTIE.

BERTIE. Why don't you come inside out of the sun, you'll feel much better for it.

He helps her towards the house.

MURIEL. Yes, you're right, I can't take the heat like I used to.

MURIEL *goes with* BERTIE *up the steps to the house. She looks quizzically at* DAPHNE *and* LYDIA. *She does not remember a thing.*

LYDIA. She doesn't mean anything by it, she's very ill. I don't suppose she knows what she's doing half the time.

DAPHNE. She's wrong you know. I knew exactly what I was getting myself into. Everyone warned me of course, parents and friends. But I didn't care, well you don't at that age, do you? And we were happy. He never promised anything and I didn't expect it. You see, there was always only ever going to be one ending, but when it came I wasn't ready for it. I didn't get to say goodbye, and I deserved that, he never told me he was going. One minute he was there, then he was gone. I suppose he thought he was making it easier for me but we knew it wouldn't be . . . That was my time! I needed it. I wanted that pain, and he robbed me of it. I'll never forgive him for that.

LYDIA. Perhaps he didn't want to see you upset?

DAPHNE. That was the price he should have paid.

MR JONES *goes over to* LYDIA *and* DAPHNE. *He places in their hands jasmine petals he has collected off the bush. They both take them and smell them. Slow fade to black out.*

Scene Two

Evening, the garden is now completely dressed for the dance with fairy lights, Chinese lanterns and bunting. There are extra chairs scattered about. At the base of the stairs there is a trestle table with drinks. There is a plinth, draped with the Union flag, on which there sits the bust of Field Marshal Lord Roberts with a quoit around his neck. From the house we hear the song 'Cherry Pink and Apple Blossom White'. VIOLET, who is dressed in an awful pink dress with ribbons, is lighting the lanterns. She sashays over to the table and pours herself a large whiskey and soda. Suddenly all the lights go out, and the music groans slowly to a stop. All is dark except for the light thrown out from the Chinese lanterns. We can hear the sound of crickets.

VIOLET. Oh for goodness sake! Daphne! Daphne! The lights have gone.

DAPHNE (*from off-stage*). We'll be with you in a minute, don't panic!

VIOLET. Who's panicking! (*To herself.*) Just because the bloody natives can't keep the lights on? ... Bloody lunatics running the asylum, if you ask me.

She goes over to the drinks table and pours herself another drink. She puts a little in first, then fills it up.

VIOLET. Sod the chota peg, mine's a large one.

MR JONES *comes out with two candelabras. He wears his usual suit. He's followed by* LYDIA, *who carries two oil lamps. She wears a cocktail dress and looks very smart, which* VIOLET *cannot help but notice. She adjusts her own dress.*

JONES. Here we are, all is not lost.

VIOLET. It's typical, the moment we decide to have a little fun, they cut the power.

JONES. I don't think it's personal, Violet.

VIOLET. I wouldn't be so sure. I might have to get my grandfather's pistol. You never know, it could be 1857 all over again!

MURIEL *comes down the steps dressed in an evening gown.*

MURIEL. Considering we take such pride in our space programme, it seems almost criminal that we can't go twenty-four hours without a sodding power cut. Violet, pour me a milk punch.

She goes over to the other chairs near the gate and sits down. VIOLET *goes over and pours her drink from the punch bowl.*

VIOLET. Lydia, milk punch?

LYDIA. No, thank you, I've still some things to do.

VIOLET. Mr Jones, milk punch or a peg?

JONES. Just a chotah peg for me.

He wanders over to the jasmine plant by the wall and starts to pick the blossoms. VIOLET *starts to make the drinks. She's a bit tiddly now.*

VIOLET. A milk punch for Muriel and a chotah peg for Mr Jones. Soda or water?

JONES. Soda please.

VIOLET. Soda for Mr Jones. And not forgetting one large peg for Violet. Here we are.

She turns to hand him his drink, not knowing he's moved away.

VIOLET. Where's the bugger gone?

JONES. Over here.

VIOLET *goes over to him and hands over his drink.*

JONES. Cheers.

VIOLET. Chin-chin. Would you take this drink over to Muriel? I'm going to ask Daphne if we can borrow her gramophone, we can't have a dance without music.

JONES. What a splendid idea.

He takes the drink and VIOLET *goes off into the house.* MR JONES *goes over to* MURIEL.

JONES. Here you are Muriel.

MURIEL. Thanks, where's Violet?

JONES. Gone to ask Daphne if we can use her gramophone while the electricity's off.

MURIEL. Oh well, better than no music at all. Do watch her though, you know how giddy she gets. I think we've some old 78's in the storeroom. Better tell Elliot to get them out. Elliot!

JONES. I'll fetch them.

MURIEL. No, no you sit and finish your drink. There's goodness knows what lurking in there . . . Elliot! . . . last time Bertie went in he was chased out by a King cobra.

DAPHNE *comes out onto the verandah; she is putting on some earrings.*

DAPHNE. Muriel, what is it? Elliot's not here. Did you want something?

MURIEL. It doesn't matter. Something from the storeroom.

DAPHNE. Violet's rummaging about in there now.

MURIEL. Tell her to be careful because . . .

DAPHNE. Don't worry, she's got her sabre. Listen out for the gate bell, people should be arriving by now.

DAPHNE *goes back into the house.*

JONES. We did say 8.30?

MR JONES *looks at his watch and wanders over to the gate.*

JONES. People just don't seem to be punctual any more, in my day it would be very bad form to be late . . . Mind you, it was just as bad to be early . . . It's very quiet out there tonight.

MURIEL. As children, we used to get so excited when there was a dance. It was so magical. Watching everyone arriving. The women looking so elegant in their beautiful dresses and all the men in black tie . . . I would always be allowed to help fasten my mother's necklace with my father, my hands in his. I can still smell his cologne when he kissed me goodnight. Mother loathed it. 'Made him smell like a native', she said. Years later, I found out that her grandfather used to wear it. He'd been born and bred in 'Black Town' Sided with the mutineers in '57 and went native. Turned up years later as a wandering fakir selling herbal remedies. Daddy told me it was especially blended for the Emperor Shah Jehan and he'd rub a little behind my ears. Such a handsome man . . . I've been thinking of them so much lately. I miss them . . . strange, I haven't done that in years.

MR JONES *hasn't really been listening; he comes over from the gate.*

JONES. Perhaps it's the power cut, maybe they're waiting for the lights to come back on.

MURIEL. Did you ever go to Firpos?

JONES. Oh, no, it was far too swish for me.

MURIEL. Yes, very swish if you could pass. It seems so silly now that such store was set by the shade of your skin. My mother used to say 'Don't get a tan, cover yourself up or you'll end up looking like a jungli.' Do you know she used to scrub her elbows with a toothbrush and bleach!

JONES. I had an aunt who did the same, 'Elbows and knees always give you away' she said. 'They'll spot you coming a mile off.'

MURIEL. I couldn't have cared less, walked around without a hat all the time, black as a sweeper. Probably why I didn't catch me a Tommy during the war. Oh, they were an ugly lot. Hot, sweaty and red-faced from the sun. Always trying to paw you. Still, they were a ticket to Blighty I suppose. My friend, Victoria Holland, married one. Her father had done very well in the customs office. They had a lovely flat in Lindsay Street, masses of servants. Her chap was a sergeant in the Durham Light Infantry and she ended up in a miner's cottage in the middle of nowhere.

JONES. Durham, Durham on the Weir!

MURIEL. Newcastle, Newcastle on the Tyne!

JONES. London, London on the Thames!

They both start to laugh. VIOLET *comes out carrying an old wind-up gramophone and a case full of records.*

VIOLET. Calcutta, Calcutta on the bloody Hooghly! Look what I've got, what shall we hear first?

JONES. Surprise us.

VIOLET *starts to rifle through a box of records, looking for something to play.*

MURIEL. What in heavens name is she wearing?

JONES. She got the pattern from a magazine, I believe it's a Hartnell. He dresses the Queen.

MURIEL. Well unless the Queen of England's taken to dressing like the Easter Bunny, I fear Violet's calculations have gone awry.

JONES. Oh, don't say anything, she's been working at it for weeks.

VIOLET has now found the record she wants to play. She starts to wind up the gramophone and places the record on the turntable and lets down the needle. We hear the strains of 'Brazil' sung by Don Marino Barreto and his Cuban Orchestra. She dances over to MR JONES.

VIOLET. Mr Jones, how's your Samba?

MURIEL. I think I'm going to need another drink.

JONES. Probably as scratchy as this record.

VIOLET. Nonsense, come on, let's cut a rug. Muriel, mine's a large peg while you're at it.

She grabs MR JONES *and they start to dance.* MURIEL *goes over to the drinks' table and gets herself another milk punch; she watches them and smiles.* BERTIE *comes down the stairs dressed in a dinner jacket.*

MURIEL. Well don't you look the swanky one.

BERTIE. What do you think you're doing?

MURIEL. Getting myself a drink. Do you want a peg?

BERTIE. No, I want this dance.

MURIEL. In my condition, you might joggle what's left of my brains and finish me off!

BERTIE. Nonsense, your tumour will throb to that Latino beat.

MURIEL. Flattery will get you everywhere.

She goes with him and they start to dance.

VIOLET. Muriel, I tell you, Mr Jones has got the moves man. (*To* MR JONES.) It's a good job you weren't around when I was a young girl or I'd have eaten you alive.

JONES. You'd have had to fight my Harriet.

VIOLET. My first husband was the same, such a jealous man. He was always punching people on the nose if he thought they were looking at me in the wrong way. You never knew what to expect from one minute to the next . . . It was all terribly exciting. Braaaziiil la, la, la, la, la, la, la, laaaaa. De, de, de, de, de, de, de, deeeee. I like that in a man.

As they dance we hear loud banging on the back gate, which at first nobody hears. It gets louder. MR JONES *notices it and breaks off dancing and goes to answer it.*

JONES (*to* VIOLET). I think our guests are arriving.

VIOLET. Oh good. Fresh blood.

They both walk over to the gate, and MR JONES *opens it.* ELLIOT *falls through almost into his arms. His face is battered and bloody, and his clothes are ripped to shreds.* VIOLET *screams, which stops the others dancing.*

JONES. Oh dear god! Whatever's happened to you boy? Bertie, quick, help me carry him!

BERTIE *rushes over and between them they manage to get him into one of the chairs.*

BERTIE. Violet, stop that whimpering and get Daphne quick! Now! Move woman!

VIOLET *rushes over to the verandah and starts to shout for* DAPHNE. ELLIOT *is crying and picking at his torn clothes.*

VIOLET. Daphne! Daphne! Come quickly, somebody's throttled Elliot, Daphne!

ELLIOT. Look what they did to my party clothes.

MURIEL. Never mind your bloody clothes you silly bugger, who did this to you?

ELLIOT *is not listening to her. He gently starts to feel his head.*

ELLIOT. My head hurts, I think they cut my hair an' all.

BERTIE. Who attacked you? Elliot, listen to me. Who's done this?

ELLIOT. I don't know, they're rioting around the airport. Noo, look at my pants yaar!

DAPHNE *and* LYDIA *come running out, followed by* VIOLET *with a bowl of water,* LYDIA *carries a first aid box.*

VIOLET. You see I told you, throttled he is.

DAPHNE *starts to examine him.*

DAPHNE. Elliot keep still, let me have a look at you.

MURIEL. Well that explains the lack of enthusiasm for the dance.

ELLIOT. There's a curfew, they're rioting. Ouch you're hurting me.

MURIEL. Don't be such a ninny.

JONES. Who's rioting? Hindus? Muslims?

ELLIOT. No, the students have taken to the streets and are fighting. That fellow from Bombay couldn't even get off the plane. Mr Chakravatty and his people were waiting to greet him when the students attacked. The whole thing's just spread.

MURIEL. Did they think you were with Chakravatty?

ELLIOT. No, I told them I was on my way to see a friend and I had nothing to do with those fascists. I told them I was a cook-cum-cabaret artist but they thought I was a malc prostitute and beat me anyway.

BERTIE. Were you gallivanting round the cemetery up to your old tricks?

ELLIOT. No. I was . . . I'd just gone out for a while, to see a friend.

BERTIE. Oh Elliot, you'd promised me you'd finished with that life.

DAPHNE. Oh Bertie, shut up about the bloody cemetery! Elliot, where's the fighting now?

ELLIOT. It's all over the place, completely out of control. I barely escaped with my life.

DAPHNE. They may come here. We ought to be careful.

LYDIA. Why should they want to come here?

MURIEL. Party bloody headquarters next door. If that place goes up, we'll all go with it.

DAPHNE. Mr Jones, would you bolt the front gate please.

BERTIE. I'll go and lock the back gate.

BERTIE goes into the house.

MURIEL. Daphne, why don't you ring the police station, Sergeant Patel likes you, he may send an officer down if you ask him nicely. Go on, I'll see to Elliot.

DAPHNE. Well if you think it'll help.

DAPHNE goes off into the house.

VIOLET. I'm going get my grandfather's pistol and I'll shoot the first bugger who comes through that gate.

MURIEL. Perhaps you should give it to Bertie, Violet. He was in the army.

JONES. That should hold them back, it's quite a strong bolt. How are you doing there Elliot?

He goes over and sits with him.

VIOLET. Oh, very well, but no one gets my sabre. Got a Pataan dagger if you fancy it Lydia, take one of the buggers with you.

LYDIA. I hope it won't come to that.

VIOLET. Well I hope so too, but you have to be prepared. Be no stopping them now they've tasted blood. Bertie should get up on the wall and pot a few of the ringleaders. Just like we used to do in the old days. That usually puts the wind up them.

VIOLET *goes off into the house.*

ELLIOT. Miss Buller-Hughes, if the house is attacked, could you try and save my cabaret costumes, they're all I have.

LYDIA. Don't worry, I shouldn't think that'll happen.

ELLIOT. Yes madam, it'll go beyond the students and Mr Chakravatty now.

MURIEL. He's right, a lot of people will be out to settle old scores tonight. Don't worry though, we should be quite safe . . . Lydia, Bertie told me that I was very rude to you the other day, I must apologise. It's just that . . .

LYDIA. I understand.

MURIEL. Thank you, I'll go and see if Bertie needs any help.

MURIEL goes off into the house passing DAPHNE *as she comes out.*

MURIEL. Did Sergeant Patel say anything?

DAPHNE. No, just that they're trying to get people off the streets. There's been fourteen deaths reported so far. They can't spare any officers to come down here, he told us to lock all the doors and sit tight.

MURIEL goes into the house. VIOLET *comes out of the house with her pistol; she also has the sabre strapped to her waist.*

VIOLET. Here we are, it needs a bit of a clean, but it should do.

We hear the door rattle. VIOLET, LYDIA, DAPHNE, MR JONES *and* ELLIOT *all look at it.*

JONES (*whispered*). Lydia quick, go and fetch Bertie! You others get over to the verandah.

He stealthily walks over to the door and tries to look through. VIOLET *has followed him over.*

JONES. Violet get back to the verandah now!

The jasmine on the wall starts to rustle and move. VIOLET *hears it. She shouts out, turns, raises her pistol and fires at the direction of the noise.*

VIOLET. Alarm! Alarm! We're under attack! Remember Cawnpore!

She shoots again. She runs over to the wall firing.

JONES. Violet!

We hear a yelp come from behind the wall. ELLIOT *screams,* LYDIA, BERTIE, MURIEL *come running from the house.* VIOLET *is shooting off rounds.*

CHAKRA. Don't shoot! Please don't shoot!

LYDIA. My god! That sounds like Mr Chakravatty!

DAPHNE. Violet, stop shooting!

ELLIOT. My costumes! My costumes!

BERTIE. Violet! Cease fire at once!

JONES. Hand over that weapon!

VIOLET. I think I got one of the buggers!

MURIEL. Elliot, will you stop that racket!

BERTIE. Give me that bloody pistol now! Are you stark raving mad woman? You could have killed someone.

VIOLET *seems quite happy with this.*

VIOLET. Yes, I think I did. (*She draws out her sabre.*) And if I didn't, I'll go finish the bugger off with this.

MR JONES *takes it out of her hand.*

JONES. Oh no you don't.

DAPHNE. Careful, she's got a dagger as well.

VIOLET. We're being attacked.

MR CHAKRAVATTY'S *face appears at the top of the wall looking very scared. He clambers over, his clothes are dirty and torn, he carries a suitcase, his face is battered and bloody. He has a wound on the arm from the shot fired at him by* VIOLET. *He is very scared. He flattens himself against the wall unsure how they will treat him.*

CHAKRA. Don't shoot, please it's me Chakravatty, I beg you.

DAPHNE. We're so sorry Mr Chakravatty, we thought you were the mob.

BERTIE. Are you alright, she didn't hit you, did she?

CHAKRA. No, no, it's just a scratch.

VIOLET *seems quite pleased that she hit something.*

VIOLET. Told you I'd winged him. It's a good job they spotted you before I got over that wall with my sabre or you'd have been a gonner, I'm telling you man.

CHAKRA. You've got to help me, they're trying to murder me. Hide me please! They've killed Mr Bhose, the bank manager!

DAPHNE. No.

MURIEL. Well if you play with fire you get burnt.

BERTIE. Of course we'll hide you, what do you take us for man.

CHAKRAVATTY *is very upset by the events of the night.*

CHAKRA. It was terrible, I've never seen people behave like this. They were animals, animals.

LYDIA. Perhaps we'd better get you a drink.

JONES. I'll get it. Brandy.

BERTIE. You'd better sit down and let Daphne take a look at that arm.

DAPHNE *comes over and starts to dress his arm.*

CHAKRA. Poor Mr Bhose, I couldn't do anything. They just grabbed him and pulled him into the crowd, I was helpless. They just cut him to pieces.

DAPHNE. Oh the poor man.

CHAKRA. He'd just been made area manager.

He breaks down and cries. The others don't quite know what to do, they just stand there and watch him.

BERTIE. Now, now, come along old chap, you don't want to go upsetting yourself.

DAPHNE. Yes, there was nothing you could have done. You mustn't blame yourself.

VIOLET. Yes, yes, it's true, he should have been a lot quicker on his feet, especially in a riot.

JONES. Violet.

MURIEL *is standing listening to all this.*

CHAKRA. He was screaming, and I . . . we couldn't help him! I tried to talk to them but they were possessed they . . . they tore him apart.

JONES. Poor fellow.

CHAKRA. I just ran, the streets are full of madness, people screaming, fires all over. How could this have happened? I'm a man of peace, you know me, I never wanted anything like this!

BERTIE. What about the other people you were with?

CHAKRA. I don't know. It all happened so quickly.

He gets up; he does not know where to go.

Perhaps I should leave, they're coming here, I know they are. They want me, they were calling my name. They want to kill me too.

BERTIE. Listen, they won't dream of looking for you here, and if they did, we'd never give you away man.

JONES. Of course we wouldn't.

CHAKRA. I have money you know, I can pay you, just allow me to stay here till morning.

DAPHNE. Mr Chakravatty, we don't want your money, you can stay as long as you like.

CHAKRA. It was a peaceful gathering and we were set upon, attacked from all sides!

JONES. Come along man, why don't we go inside and you can swill your face. You'll feel so much better for it. Come along now.

CHAKRAVATTY *goes with him into the house.*

BERTIE. Well, he seems to have stirred up a right bloody hornet's nest tonight. What a terrible waste of life, god they make me sick.

MURIEL. Then put him out, let him feel what it's like to be hunted down.

LYDIA. I think he knows that now.

MURIEL. No, these people never learn, next week he'll be back in the bazaar stirring them up again. Oh he's shocked and scared now, but he'll build on it, use it to his advantage.

BERTIE. Muriel, I wouldn't put a dog out on a night like this, nobody's safe. I don't agree with his politics either but there are limits.

MURIEL. Do you think he would do the same for you? Do you think he would feel any pang of remorse about taking this house away from us and seeing us on the streets? Well do you?

BERTIE. But we're not like him are we, it's not the way we think, it's not the way we were brought up to behave.

MURIEL. Oh Bertie, stop being so bloody British! Perhaps that's our problem, we should've been more like them. Perhaps we should behave exactly like Chakravatty. Maybe we worshipped the wrong culture all these years, maybe his gods are stronger. So let's put them to the test, let's see if they save him tonight!

DAPHNE. Muriel you're being ridiculous! You know yourself no one can be blamed for these situations, they start from nothing.

ELLIOT. It was his people who started the trouble in the bazaar. They burnt a Muslim man they found near the temple.

CHAKRAVATTY *has come out onto the balcony with* MR JONES.

CHAKRA. No, it wasn't like that at all, why are you lying about this? It was a completely unprovoked attack. My people were the victims.

ELLIOT. Don't believe him! He's a murderer.

CHAKRA. How dare you say that to me you degenerate! Tonight my members became martyrs. They blessed the ground with their blood.

MURIEL. How much of your hatred and poison do you think people would take? You're not concerned for their welfare, all you want is power, power at any cost, and you don't care how many people die in gaining it for you. You call them animals, but you're the animals, you're obscene. You pervert your religion and infect people's minds with your fanatical bigotry.

In the distance, but getting louder, we can here the mob's approach. CHAKRAVATTY *starts to get very nervous. He tries to speak to them but they turn or look away.*

CHAKRA. We have rights as well! We are ignored because we have shoes on our feet and clothes on our back, because by birth we are of a higher caste. For years we have been made to feel ashamed of our birthright but no more. We are being swamped. We have declared a caste war. Tonight showed that we cannot treat these people as fellow citizens, they can't enjoy the same rights as we do. (*He starts to falter.*) Not when, when . . . they put their god above their country . . . or, or, when they behave like this to their countrymen . . . they're filth from the lowest castes who want to break down our morals, (*Beat.*) abuse our beliefs, soil our caste with their shadows . . . they, they . . . pollute . . . we have . . .

He knows it is useless, he knows they see through him.

BERTIE. Mr Chakravatty, you may stay here as long as you wish, but please refrain from spewing out any more of that rubbish or by god, I'll throw you to the crowd myself.

MURIEL. You'd let him stay here after . . .

BERTIE. Not now Muriel, can't you see the man is . . .

MURIEL. If not now, when? The streets are filled with hatred incited by this man and people like him. He's fine, he's safe here, it's those out there that are dying.

CHAKRA. I am always ready to die for my beliefs.

MURIEL. Are you Mr Chakravatty, are you really? Is that why you crawled in here to hide with us.

CHAKRA. I would defend my religion to my last breath.

MURIEL. The army of the gods you call yourselves, but you forget that when you call on gods they demand a sacrifice. And Mr Bhose? Was that enough to appease them, or will they want more? What else are you going to give them Mr Chakravatty, who else can you spare?

CHAKRAVATTY *is now backing away from* MURIEL.

CHAKRA. None of this was supposed to happen! It's not what I wanted, I told them we weren't ready for this yet!

MURIEL. What about you Mr Chakravatty, will they sacrifice you tonight?

CHAKRA. Nooo! Get her away from me! Please help me!

The mob is outside the doors of the house.
CHAKRAVATTY *starts to back away.*

JONES. Muriel for god's sake, stop it!

CHAKRA. I should have known not to trust you people, that you'd sell me out to the scum out there. I've got to get away from here.

The noise of the crowd is at fever pitch. Suddenly we hear a whush and MR CHAKRAVATTY's *house goes up in flames bathing the stage in a red glow, the crowd cheer. We hear the sound of the sarangi, a type of Indian violin, which gets louder and louder as the flames flicker across the stage.*

DAPHNE. My god, they've torched the house!

CHAKRAVATTY *shouts to the crowd.*

CHAKRA. Get away from there! Get away from my house, I'll kill you all!

BERTIE. For god's sake man stay here!

BERTIE *tries to get hold of him but* CHAKRAVATTY *snatches up the gun off the table. He starts to back away towards the garden wall.*

CHAKRA. Stay away from me! I'll use this!

JONES. If you go outside they'll rip you to shreds!

MURIEL. No, go! Your god's are calling you! Can't you hear them, listen! Listen they're calling your name. Go, go now! Quickly!

CHAKRAVATTY *looks wildly round at them, he's crying, the mob is shouting, the music is reaching a crescendo and the stage is bathed in a red flickering glow as the flames devour his house. He runs and scrambles over the wall, we hear a roar from the crowd, we hear two shots fired. We hear a piercing scream from* CHAKRAVATTY. BERTIE *rushes over to the wall with a chair and stands on it to see what's happening.*

BERTIE. Oh dear god, they're going to throw him into the house.

The crowd becomes hysterical. We hear terrible screams from CHAKRAVATTY *which eventually peter out.* BERTIE *turns and sits on the chair. The sound of the crowd drifts away, as does the sound of the sarangi. The others stand in shock,* DAPHNE *holds her hands up to her face,* LYDIA *sits down into a chair.* MURIEL *suddenly seems to crumple slowly to the floor.* DAPHNE *and the others rush over to her.* BERTIE *has her in his lap and holds up her head.*

BERTIE. Oh, Muriel not now! Mr Jones, call the doctor quickly!

MR JONES *runs into the house.*

MURIEL. I'm sorry my love, I don't think I have the choice this time.

BERTIE. No, I won't let you!

MURIEL. What a bloody dance eh?

MURIEL *seems to go limp in* BERTIE*'s arms. The power comes back on, and the record player in the house slurs to life. It's still playing 'Cherry Pink and Apple Blossom White'. The lights fade to black.*

Curtain.

The End.

A Nick Hern Book

Last Dance at Dum Dum first published in Great Britain
in 1999 as a paperback original by Nick Hern Books Ltd,
14 Larden Road, London W3 7ST in association with
the Royal Court Theatre and the Ambassador Theatre Group,
London

Last Dance at Dum Dum copyright © 1999 Ayub Khan-Din

Ayub Khan-Din has asserted his right to be identified as the
author of this work

ISBN 1 85459 456 7

A CIP catalogue record for this book is available from the
British Library

Typeset by Country Setting, Kingsdown, Kent CT14 8ES

Printed and bound in Great Britain by Cox & Wyman Ltd,
Reading, Berks

Amateur Performing Rights   Applications for performance,
including readings and excerpts, by amateurs in the English
language throughout the world (except in the United States of
America and Canada) should be made before rehearsals begin
to Nick Hern Books, 14 Larden Road, London W3 7ST, *fax* +
44 (0) 20-8746-2006, *e-mail* info@nickhernbooks.demon.co.uk

Professional Performing Rights   Applications for
performance by professionals in any medium and in any
language throughout the world (and by amateurs in the United
States of America and Canada) should be addressed to
Sebastian Born, The Agency (London) Ltd, 24 Pottery Lane,
London W11 4LZ, *fax* +44 (0) 20-7727-9037